# ROMAN
# LEGIONARIES

## SOLDIERS OF EMPIRE

Simon Elliott

**CASEMATE**

*Oxford & Philadelphia*

Published in Great Britain and
the United States of America in 2018 by
CASEMATE PUBLISHERS
The Old Music Hall, 106–108 Cowley Road, Oxford OX4 1JE, UK
1950 Lawrence Road, Havertown, PA 19083, USA

Paperback Edition: ISBN 978-1-61200-611-6
Digital Edition: ISBN 978-1-61200-612-3 (epub)

A CIP record for this book is available from the British Library

Printed in the Czech Republic by FINIDR, s.r.o.

Typeset in India by Versatile PreMedia Services. www.versatilepremedia.com

For a complete list of Casemate titles, please contact:

CASEMATE PUBLISHERS (UK)
Telephone (01865) 241249
Email: casemate-uk@casematepublishers.co.uk
www.casematepublishers.co.uk

CASEMATE PUBLISHERS (US)
Telephone (610) 853-9131
Fax (610) 853-9146
Email: casemate@casematepublishers.com
www.casematepublishers.com

# CONTENTS

# INTRODUCTION

The Roman legionary was the elite fighting soldier of the ancient world. Clad in helmet and banded iron armour, and carrying rectangular body shield, lead-weighted javelins and vicious stabbing sword, his image has come to symbolise the might of the Roman Empire.

The story of how this warrior rose to the pinnacle of martial prowess is a more complex one than commonly thought. To a large extent it reflects the Roman trait for the successful assimilation of their opponents' best military ideas, a thread examined in detail in this work. This, together with Roman society's unusual propensity for 'grit' with its seeming inability to accept defeat in any form, meant that those who stood toe-to-toe on the battlefield with the Roman legionary were brave indeed, or foolish.

Much has been written about the Roman legionary, and this book both builds on that canon of work but also brings my own new primary research about the Roman military to the fore. In so doing it tells the legionary's story for a new generation, one perhaps keener than ever to understand the wider experience of life as a Roman warrior on the frontiers of this most imperial of empires as it waxed inexorably, and then waned dramatically. In that context it shows how the Roman legionary and his role in battle changed from one always on the front foot, driving the borders of the empire forward with unstoppable legionary spearheads, to one acting as the bulwark on the Roman *limes* as offence turned to defence, the empire's enemies now crashing upon her borders.

To tell this dramatic story the book is broken down into five chapters (and a conclusion), each sequentially building the reader's knowledge of every aspect of the Roman legionary's life. This introduction sets the scene for the book. Chapter 1 provides a brief narrative on the history of the mid-later Roman Republic and then the Principate and Dominate phases of the empire, to allow the reader to see how the legionary sat within the wider context of Roman society and history. The next three chapters form the core of the book, covering the history of the Roman legionary and detailing his equipment, then the legionary on campaign and in battle, and finally the legionary in his many non-conflict related roles. The latter reflects the numerous specialists within the legions of Rome over and above the fighting troops, which allowed the Roman state to deploy the military for a wide variety of tasks additional to their more obvious role as the cutting edge of Roman military power. The main focus here is the Principate legionary of the 2nd and early 3rd centuries AD when the empire was at its height. Next, I briefly look at other Roman troop types which, together with the legionary, made up the overall Roman military complement. This peaked at around 450,000 as the reign of Septimius Severus came to an end in AD 211 (in 33 legions and around 400 auxiliary units). In the same chapter I also consider the later Roman army of the Dominate to

A **legionary** was the elite fighting soldier of the mid–late Roman Republic, the Principate Empire, and at least the early part of the Dominate Empire. An **auxiliary** was a lesser though still professional fighting soldier of the Principate and Dominate Empires. Naval *milites* (a generic name for soldier) refers to all nautical troops in the fleets of Rome, whether marines, sailors or rowers.

show how the role of the legionary changed as the military evolved to face rapidly evolving threats from both without and within. Finally the book ends with my conclusion, considering the legacy of the Roman legionary in terms of military tradition, and also our wider appreciation of the Roman Republic and Empire.

When using classical and modern names, I have attempted to ensure the research presented on the legionary and the Roman military more broadly is as accessible as possible to the reader. For example, I use the modern name where a place is mentioned, referencing its Roman name (if appropriate) at that first point of usage. Meanwhile, when a classical name for a role or position is well understood such as *legate*, I use that (referencing the modern name at the first use, in this case general).

The size-based hierarchy for **permanent fortifications** now utilised by those studying the armed forces of Rome to describe their size describes:

- Fortress, a permanent base for one or more legions. Some were 20 hectares or more in size, a significant engineering undertaking for the legionaries and other military units of Rome.
- Vexillation fortress, a large fort of between eight and 12 hectares. Such fortifications held a mixed force of legionary cohorts and auxiliaries.
- Fort, a garrison outpost occupied by an auxiliary unit or units. These were between one and six hectares in size.
- Fortlet, a small garrison outpost large enough to hold only part of an auxiliary unit.

Temporary fortifications in the form of marching camps, built by a Roman military force at the end of every day's march in enemy territory, were also a key feature of the professional life of the legionary.

**TIMELINE**

| | |
|---|---|
| **509 BC** | Rome becomes a republic. |
| **404 BC** | The siege of Veii begins. |
| **401 BC** | Marcus Furius Camillus becomes consular tribune, and later introduces the manipular system into the Roman army. |
| **280 BC** | The Battle of Heraclea, where Roman legionaries come up against Hellenistic phalanxes for first time. |
| **107 BC** | Gaius Marius becomes consul for the first time. During his consulships he makes changes to the Roman army, known as the Marian reforms. |
| **58 BC** | Julius Caesar begins his conquest of Gaul. |
| **57 BC** | The Veneti submit to Caesar. |
| **56 BC** | The rebellion of the Veneti against Rome, battle of Morbihan. |
| **55 BC** | The first Roman invasion of Britain, Julius Caesar's first incursion. |
| **54 BC** | The second Roman invasion of Britain, Julius Caesar's second incursion. |
| **52 BC** | The battle of Alesia. Conquest of Gaul completed. |
| **44 BC** | Julius Caesar assassinated in Rome. |
| **27 BC** | The conquest of north-west Spain begins. Octavian becomes Augustus. Beginning of the Principate Empire. |
| **AD 9** | Varus' three legions, together with nine auxiliary units, destroyed in Teutoburg Forest, Germany by the Cherusci tribe and others led by Arminius. |
| **AD 43** | The third Roman invasion of Britain under Claudius. |
| **AD 60/61** | The Boudiccan Revolt. |
| **AD 197/198** | Severus begins his reforms of the military, while he himself campaigns in Parthia for two years. |

| | |
|---|---|
| **AD 202** | Severus campaigns in North Africa. |
| **AD 209** | First Severan campaign in Scotland. |
| **AD 210** | Second Severan campaign in Scotland. |
| **AD 224** | Ardashir I of Persia defeats his Parthian overlords over a two-year period, bringing the Sassanid Persian Empire into being. Rome now has a fully symmetrical threat on her eastern border. |
| **AD 235** | Assassination of Severus Alexander, ending the Severan dynasty and beginning the 'Crisis of the 3rd century'. |
| **AD 274** | Emperor Aurelian defeats the 'Gallic Empire', with Britain, Gaul and Spain then rejoining the empire. |
| **AD 284** | Emperor Diocletian initiates the Diocletianic reforms of the military. The end of the 'Crisis of the 3rd century'. |
| **AD 293** | The western caesar Constantius Chlorus recaptures northern Gaul from Carausius. |
| **AD 296** | The fourth Roman invasion of Britain, with Constantius Chlorus invading to defeat Allectus. |
| **AD 306** | Constantine is proclaimed emperor in York by the legionaries of legio VI Victrix. |
| **AD 312** | Constantine becomes the sole emperor in the west, with his military reforms beginning around this time. |
| **AD 314** | Constantine and Licinius agree to end the persecution of Christians. |
| **AD 324** | Constantine becomes the sole emperor of the whole empire. |
| **AD 325** | The first mention of *comitatenses* field army troops. |
| **AD 337** | Constantine prepares for war with Persia but falls ill in Nicomedia and dies. |
| **AD 350** | The military leader Magnentius (born in Britain) usurps power in Gaul, with the |

provinces in Britain and Spain quickly supporting him, and ultimately the whole of the Western Empire.

**AD 351**  Magnentius is defeated by the Eastern Emperor Constantius II at the battle of Mursa Major, he then retreats to Gaul. Magnentius is defeated again at the battle of Mons Seleucus, after which he commits suicide.

**AD 357**  The battle of Strasbourg, where Julian defeats the Alamanni.

**AD 378**  The battle of Adrianople: the eastern armies of the Emperor Valens are defeated by the Gothic army of Fritigern, a defeat the empire struggles to recover from.

**AD 383**  Magnus Maximus, the British military commander, and possibly the *vicarius* of the diocese, campaigns against Pictish and Irish raiders. He is proclaimed emperor by his troops, then invades Gaul which declares its support for him, as does Spain.

**AD 387**  Magnus Maximus invades Italy where he ousts the emperor, Valentinian II.

**AD 388**  Magnus Maximus is defeated and executed by Theodosius I, emperor in the East.

**AD 391**  Theodosius I bans pagan worship.

**AD 405**  Heavy Irish raiding on the southwestern coast of Britain occurs, this being a possible date for the capture of St Patrick.

**AD 406**  Vandals, Burgundians, Alans, Franks and Suevi overrun the *limes Germanicus* near Mainz and then invade Gaul.

**AD 407**  In swift succession the military in Britain declare Marcus, then Gratian and finally Constantine III to be the emperor. The latter crosses to Gaul with the remaining comitatenses field army troops from Britain, setting up his capital at Arles. The diocese now only has the limitanei troops to defend its borders.

| AD 409 | The British aristocracy throw out their Roman administrators, with the diocese cut adrift from the remaining parts of the Western Empire. |
| AD 411 | Constantine III is captured and executed on the orders of Honorius. |
| AD 476 | The last western emperor, Romulus Augustulus, is deposed by his *magister militum* Flavius Odaocer. The end of the Roman Empire in the west. |

## Roman Emperors to AD 211

| 27 BC–AD 14 | Augustus |
| AD 14–37 | Tiberius |
| AD 37–41 | Caligula |
| AD 41–54 | Claudius |
| AD 54–68 | Nero |
| AD 68–69 | Galba |
| AD 69 | The Year of Four Emperors: Galba, Otho, Vitellius, Vespasian |
| AD 69–79 | Vespasian |
| AD 79–81 | Titus |
| AD 81–96 | Domitian |
| AD 96–98 | Nerva |
| AD 98–117 | Trajan |
| AD 117–138 | Hadrian |
| AD 138–161 | Antoninus Pius |
| AD 161–169 | Marcus Aurelius and Lucius Verus |
| AD 169–180 | Marcus Aurelius |
| AD 177–192 | Commodus |
| AD 193 | The Year of the Five Emperors |
| AD 193–211 | Septimius Severus |

# CHAPTER 1

---

# REPUBLIC AND EMPIRE

The Roman legionary is so well known to us today that it is easy for us to take his eventual appearance and rise to dominance for granted. His origins however were complex, especially given the unique panoply associated with such troops, and have their roots deep within the Roman Republic.

## Early Rome

Rome's rise to greatness was never guaranteed and was a painstaking process featuring many setbacks. These challenges were interspersed with long periods of consolidation. It was during the latter that Rome assimilated many of the ideas – both cultural and practical – of its opponents, an ability that helps explain its longevity in both republic and later empire. This trend is particularly evident during the former.

The origins of Rome are shrouded in myth. The most familiar is that of Romulus and Remus, the twins suckled by a she-wolf who decided to build a settlement. After an argument the former killed the latter and so the founding took his name. Roman annalists traditionally dated this to 21 April 753 BC. Reflecting the complexities of Roman culture however, this legend also had to be reconciled with another founding myth for the later city. This was set much earlier in time in the context of the Trojan Wars, with Trojan refugee Aeneas escaping to Italy and founding the line in Rome through his son Iulus, the namesake of the Julio-Claudian family. The merging of these two origin stories was most completely accomplished by the 1st-century BC poet Virgil.

However the original settlement was founded, its location was crucial to its subsequent rise to global dominance. It was one of a number built on hilltops on the left bank of the River Tiber in central Italy at its lowest crossing point. This river is one of two major waterways that rise in the central Apennine Mountains bisecting Italy. The Tiber flows south into the Tyrrhenian Sea, while the other is the River Arno, which flows west into the same sea. The region between the two, from Pisa in the north to Ostia (the port of Rome) in the south, was called Etruria and was originally home to the Villanovan iron age culture which began around 900 BC.

This evolved by the early 7th century BC into the Etruscan culture, with the growing villages of rich Etruria coalescing into powerful city states such as Caere, Veii and Tarquinii. Etruscan influence spread rapidly, largely through their seafaring skills, with a mercantile empire soon established in the western Mediterranean. Through this they soon came into contact with the Greek colonies in southern Italy and eastern Sicily, and the Phoenicians who were establishing the Punic Empire in North Africa. From the former they adopted the Greek hoplite phalanx as the principal formation of their better-armed troops. This gave them a distinctive edge as they looked south to the settlements above the eastern bank of the Tiber, including Rome, and the region to their south called Latium. Soon these were all under their control, with Rome being governed by an Etrusco-Roman king. The second of these, Servius Tullius (579–535 BC), was particularly important as he formalised the military systems of Rome for the first time, following Etruscan tradition by again introducing the hoplite phalanx for the best troops (see Chapter 2).

Etruscan power reached its height in the mid-6th century BC when they conquered much of Campania below Latium, including many of the Greek settlements of Magna Graecia. However, crucially they failed to capture the key city of

Cumae there. This formed the centre of regional resistance to Etruscan rule, defeating the latter in battle in 524 BC. The event emboldened the other conquered settlements and those in Latium formed the Latin League which, together with the Greek settlements of Magna Graecia, began to drive the Etruscans back north into Etruria. Rome's first rise to regional dominance occurred at this time when it became the principal town of the league under the reign of Tarquin the Proud (534–509 BC). He was still nevertheless Etrusco-Roman, and in 509 BC the Roman aristocracy expelled him and the Roman Republic was born. It was in the context of the latter event that we have the story of Horatio and his two companions holding the last bridge over the River Tiber from Etruscans returning to try to help Tarquin. As legend goes, their sacrifice proved worthwhile, with Tarquin the last Roman king.

# The early republic

After the fall of the monarchy the new Roman Republic came under the control of the great families of Rome, called the patricians based on the Latin word *patres* (father). It was only members of these great families that could hold religious or political office, particularly the Senate where the most important members of the nobility carried out legislation under the aegis of two annually elected consuls. The remaining citizens – known as plebeians – had no political authority, even though many were as wealthy as the patricians. Tensions between the two classes grew rapidly, particularly as the poorer residents provided the bulk of the army. In 494 BC matters came to a head when the plebeians went on strike. They gathered outside Rome and refused to move until they were granted representation, the event called the First Succession of the Plebs. Against the odds, the dramatic move worked and the plebeians were rewarded with their own assembly called the *Concillium Plebis* (Council of the Plebs). This body had a degree of oversight on the legislation proposed by the consuls and enacted by the Senate. Thus, while the government of the Roman Republic was by no means democratic (also excluding women from any public office), it was much more so than the preceding monarchy, and that became an important part of the Roman psyche.

During the early republic Roman foreign policy and military activity was often far from successful. Much of the 5th century BC was spent struggling against external threats from near and far. In the first instance Rome fought the Latin War with its erstwhile Latin League partners from 498 to 493 BC. Even though Rome was victorious in the main engagement, the battle of Regallus in 496 BC, the town had to acknowledge her Latin neighbours as equals in the subsequent Cassian Treaty.

As Etruscan power waned, the Latin League then spent much of the next 50 years fending off repeated raiding in force by the various hill tribes of the Apennines, for example the Aequi, Umbri, Sabini and Volsci. These found themselves increasingly squeezed out of their own lands and onto the plains of Latium by the expansion of the Samnites to the south and east. By the mid-5th century BC these tribes, driving all before them, burst into southern Italy and conquered Campania, Apulia and Lucania. The Latin towns led the fightback, with the Aequi defeated in 431 BC and the Volsci then driven back into the hills. The Latin League then consolidated their control over central-western Italy, with comparative peace descending on the region for a short time.

This was not to last as, to the north, the Etruscans remained a threat. They again drew the attention of Rome which, in 404 BC, began a long eight-year siege of the Etruscan city of Veii. This finally fell in 396 BC and proved to be the high point for Roman foreign policy in the first half of the 4th century BC. This was because their next opponents were the Senones Gauls from northern Italy. Here Celts from central Europe had been settling in the Po Valley for some time, challenging the Etruscans who had established Bologne as their principal city there. The riches to the south proved too strong a draw and, after bursting through Etruria, a Gallic army under Brennus found itself on the borders of Latium. Rome deployed its legions expecting a swift victory, but was shocked when they were annihilated at the battle of Allia in 390 BC. This was only 17km to the north of Rome, which was promptly sacked. The traumatic event prompted the building of the first defensive circuit of the city in the form of the 11-kilometre Servian Walls.

In the midst of these events an appointment occurred in Rome which was to have a profound effect on the development of the Roman military system, leading to the appearance of the legionary for the first time. This was the appointment of Marcus Furius Camillus as consular tribune to command the army in 401 BC. A patrician with extensive experience of campaigning against the Aequi and Volsci, he realised that Rome's incessant campaigning, which came to a head with the long siege of Veii, was proving financially unsustainable. He therefore raised taxation to a level where it could support the army on long campaigns and re-balanced the books of the Roman treasury. Then, with his Camillan reforms of the military, he introduced the manipular system into the legions of Rome with the legionary at its centre (see Chapter 2 for full detail). These developments rapidly superseded the earlier Tullian system.

## The middle republic

The new system was quickly tested, once more against the Etruscans to the north. In the mid-4th century Rome and her Latin League partners fought a series of increasingly vicious wars against the Etrurian city states. A final assault in 351 BC broke Etruscan resistance who then lost Bologne to the Gauls in 350 BC. The absence of an opponent to the north now left the towns of Latium free to look inward once more, and a final struggle for dominance of the Latin League began. Rome emerged as the victor and now controlled all of western Italy from southern Etruria to northern Campania.

By now city-sized, its next opponents were the Samnites of Samnium, an Oscan-speaking people of south central Italy used to fighting in the rough terrain of their homelands. Initially an ally of the Latin League against the Volsci, war broke out with Rome in 343 BC. This lasted for 50 years and included the famous Roman defeat at the Caudian Forks in 321 BC. This was a pass near Caudium, the capital of the Samnite Caudini tribe. Here, both Roman consuls led their combined armies into a trap where their whole force was captured, every man being forced to pass under a 'yoke' formed from three spears, two stuck in the ground and one placed horizontally over them. Rome never forgave the Samnites for this humiliation and within five years the 'Caudine Peace' had broken down, with hostilities renewed. The Samnites were for the most part victorious, but typically the Romans refused to accept defeat and tenaciously fought back. The Samnites eventually sued for peace in 304 BC. This was again short lived, lasting only six years. The Samnites then launched a full-out assault on Rome in 296 BC, gathering a coalition of allies including the Gauls, the remaining Etruscan city states and Umbrians, aiming to curb the growing of Rome once and for all. Again they were initially successful, but ultimately lost the key battle at Sentinum in 295 BC when only the Gauls turned up to fight alongside them. This marked the end of Samnite resistance to Roman expansion southwards, and also of Etruscan independence.

Rome now turned its attention to northern Italy where the Gauls still dominated. In the early 280s BC a large-scale migration took place of the Gallic peoples of central Europe and northern Italy, caused by population pressure. Huge tribal groupings began to head eastwards and south. Soon the Senone tribe were once more on the borders of Etruria, now under Roman control. In 284 BC a Roman army, 13,000 strong, marched north to intercept them but was massacred at the battle of Arretium. The Romans responded with typical grit, launching a massive counterstrike into the heart of Senonian territory in the Po Valley. After a brief struggle they evicted the whole tribe out of Italy. Another Gallic tribe, the Boii, then raided south but were fought to a standstill and sued for peace. This ended effective Gallic resistance in the north.

Rome now controlled most of the Italian peninsula excepting the Greek cities of the south, which became the next object of her attention. Rome tried to force them into an alliance, but was quickly rebuffed. Taranto, the leading naval power on the peninsula, then appealed for help from Pyrrhus of Epirus on the western coast of the Balkans. The Epirot king, a relation of Alexander the Great, responded positively and in 280 BC crossed the Adriatic with an army 25,000 strong. These crack troops fought in the Hellenistic military tradition with pikemen, lance-armed shock cavalry and war elephants. A Roman army quickly marched south when word reached the city that Pyrrhus was gathering allies from Rome's enemies across Italy. A major battle ensued at Heraclea. This was the first time the Romans, with their maniples of legionaries, fought a Macedonian-style phalanx. It was to prove a bruising experience, with Pyrrhus winning narrowly. Two further battles occurred at Asculum in 279 BC – another narrow Epirot victory – and Beneventum in 275 BC, when the Romans were finally victorious. The war had been a close-run thing though, and made a lasting impression on the Romans. One result was the evolution of the Camillan manipular system into a more streamlined form, this detailed in Chapter 2 and known as Polybian after the 2nd-century Greek historian.

Roman expansion continued and now began to take on an international flavour. By 272 BC Taranto had been captured, providing Rome with an effective maritime capability for the first time. This caused an inevitable clash with Carthage, the regional superpower of the western Mediterranean, and the First Punic War broke out in 264 BC over control over the key Sicilian city of Messina. This lasted until 241 BC and included the battle of Agrigentum on the south coast of Sicily in 261 BC where the legions of Rome defeated the Carthaginians for the first time in a set-piece battle. After this the conflict was largely naval, with the

Romans copying Carthaginian maritime technology and tactics and ending the war the victor. Carthage evacuated Sicily and paid a huge indemnity.

However it was the Second Punic War that truly tested the power and resilience of Rome to breaking point. This broke out in 218 BC and lasted 17 years, with the Roman fleet at the outset cutting off the Carthaginian North African homeland from its colonies in Spain. The Carthaginian leader Hannibal responded with his audacious plan to invade Italy through southern Gaul and the Alps, defeating the legions of Rome three times at the Trebia in 218 BC, Lake Trasimene in 217 BC and Cannae in 216 BC. The last of these was a battle of titanic scale, 50,000 Carthaginians facing 86,000 Romans. Hannibal here famously completed his famous double envelopment of the legions. A massacre followed, with 50,000 Romans being killed. Such losses would bring most opponents to their knees, but not Rome. Soon new legions were raised, including two of freed slaves. Even though most of southern Italy now defected to Hannibal, he failed to capture Rome itself and was ultimately pinned down in southern Italy. Attempts to re-supply him from North Africa and Spain failed due to Roman naval power, and in 204 BC Rome went on the offensive. This featured consul Publius Cornelius Scipio (later Africanus) landing a sizeable force of 25,000 in the Carthaginian heartland near Tunis. The legions, joined by Numidian allies, had their revenge for Cannae in 202 BC when Scipio finally defeated Hannibal at Zama. Peace quickly followed, under the most onerous terms for the Carthaginians.

The Third Punic War broke out in 146 BC with Carthage backed into a corner by the escalating demands of Rome. This was a very one-sided affair, with Carthage itself destroyed and 50,000 of its citizens sold into slavery. The event marked the beginning of Rome's mastery of the western Mediterranean, with Sicily, Sardinia and Corsica, the Balearic Islands, Spain and North Africa gradually coming under direct Roman control.

Meanwhile, an additional outcome of the Second Punic War was that Roman attention also turned to the eastern Mediterranean. Here, the Macedonian King Philip V had unwisely been caught trying to agree a treaty with Hannibal when the latter was still in Italy. The next 50 years saw the republic in conflict with the Hellenistic kingdoms and their neighbours in the Balkans, Asia Minor and Syria. These campaigns featured a number of major set-piece battles between the legions and the phalanx. The most important were Cynoscephalae in 197 BC when Philip V was defeated during the Second Macedonian War, Magnesia in 190 BC when the Seleucid king Antiochus III was defeated in the Seleucid-Roman War, and Pydna in 168 BC where the new Macedonian king Perseus was defeated. By 146 BC, with the end of the Fourth Macedonian War, the kingdom of Alexander the Great had been thoroughly defeated, with leading Achaean League city Corinth to the south suffering the same fate as Carthage and being totally destroyed. Roman power now spread throughout the region in the same manner as the western Mediterranean. The city on the left bank of the Tiber was now the undoubted super power of the ancient world, its legions triumphant across the known world.

Given the role of the aristocracy in the command of the legions it is important to understand the higher ranks of **Roman society**. In terms of the ranking of the nobility, at the top was the Senatorial class, endowed with wealth, high birth and 'moral excellence'. Next was the equestrian class, these having slightly less wealth but with a reputable lineage. Finally there was curial class, the bar set slightly lower again. Freed slaves called freedmen also played a key role in the administrations of the legions.

# The later republic

As the republic matured Rome, victorious and rich, turned on itself. First, in 133 BC tribune Tiberius Sempronius Gracchus proposed to distribute stretches of state-owned land in Italy, illegally occupied by the rich, to the poor. However, instead of following the usual practice of first consulting the Senate, he presented his idea directly to an assembly of the people. In so doing he deposed from office another tribune opposing the distribution, arguing that his reforms should be funded from the money that came from the riches now pouring into Rome from the eastern Mediterranean. His land bill passed but, when he tried to stand for election for another term, he was assassinated by a group of senators. This set the tone for all that followed in the next century.

In 123 BC Tiberius's brother Gaius was elected as a tribune, introducing a whole package of radical legislation that included state-subsidised corn rations for the population of Rome. He too was promptly murdered. Next, at the end of the century, the highly successful soldier Gaius Marius rose to the consulship, a post he then held seven times. This was an unprecedented long-term dominance of high political office by one man, setting a pattern for – effectively – warlords with private armies to control Roman public life.

Marius had been victorious against Rome's enemies in Africa, Gaul and Italy, the latter during the Social War when Rome's Italian allies revolted. He also further rationalised the military, doing away with the manipular system and building the legions anew with cohorts of similarly armed legionaries (fully detailed in Chapter 2). His success led to inevitable conflict with his political contemporaries in Rome, principally Lucius Cornelius Sulla. Another successful military leader, this time in the east, Sulla marched on Rome in 82 BC and established himself as a 'dictator'. This was an ancient Roman office, originally designed to give a leading politician short-term powers in times of crisis. Sulla held the post for two years, having thousands of his political opponents put to violent death. Unusually for such a dominant figure, he then retired from the office on his own terms and died peacefully in his bed.

The middle years of the 1st century BC were then dominated by two further individuals of great significance to the story of Rome. The first was Gnaeus Pompeius Magnus (later styled Pompey the Great), the second arguably the greatest Roman of all, Julius Caesar. Though originally allies (Pompey married Caesar's daughter Julia in 59 BC), they later became the bitterest of enemies. Both had seen great military success, Pompey in Spain and the east, Caesar in Gaul where he famously defeated the Gallic leader Vercingetorix at the siege of Alesia in 52 BC. However, they differed in their political power-bases, Pompey relying on the support of the traditionalists in the Senate while Caesar chose a populist route, following the path of radicals such as Tiberius Gracchus. Their rivalry was well recorded, particularly in the surviving letters of another contemporary politician, Marcus Tullius Cicero. Caesar himself also knew the power of a good press and made sure he recorded his victories for posterity, for example in his *Gallic War*.

Throughout most of the 50s BC Pompey and Caesar were kept in check by the First Triumvirate where Rome's richest man, Marcus Licinius Crassus, joined them to dominate public life. However Julia died in 54 BC and then, when Crassus himself was killed campaigning against the Parthians at the battle of Carrhae in 53 BC, war between the two protagonists became inevitable. First blows were struck in 49 BC, with Caesar emerging the victor at the battle of Pharsalus a year later. Pompey was later beheaded trying to land in Egypt.

Caesar now began using the title 'dictator', receiving honours usually reserved for the gods. He also embarked on a major programme of reform, including the calendar, settling landless veteran soldiers and cancelling debt. He too didn't enjoy the fruits of success for long. In 44 BC he was famously cut down in the Senate by a posse of senators keen to turn the clock back to the 'great' days of the earlier republic. Another decade of civil war followed as Caesar's supporters, led by his general Mark Antony, first of all fought his assassins, and then themselves. A brief attempt to restore peace occurred in 43 BC through the Second Triumvirate, but again this failed. War broke out once more and by 31 BC there was again only one man left standing, Caesar's nephew and adopted son Gaius Octavian, after he defeated Antony in the naval battle at Actium in northern Greece.

Octavian was keenly aware that the Roman political classes were exhausted after nearly a century of civil war, especially the recent brutal campaigns following the death of Caesar. A shrewd political operator, instead of announcing himself a 'dictator', from 27 BC he quietly started to gather the reins of power within Rome. Thus was born the Roman Empire, initially in the form of his Principate.

## The Roman Principate

This is the name given to the Roman Empire from the accession of Augustus (as Octavian now styled himself) to the end of the 'crisis of the 3rd century' when Diocletian became emperor in AD 284. The name derives from the term *princeps*, meaning chief or master, this referencing the emperor as the principal citizen of the empire. Though not an official title, it was assumed by each emperor on their accession. In reality it was a conceit, allowing the empire to be explained away as a simple continuance of the republic when in reality it was a true dictatorship.

The Principate was the period when the legionary was most recognisable to a modern audience, this period forming the backdrop for much of the detailed descriptions later in the book.

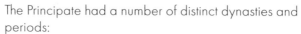

The Principate had a number of distinct dynasties and periods:

- The Julio-Claudian Dynasty, lasting from the accession of Augustus in 27 BC to the death of Nero in AD 68. This period included the beginnings of the empire, the loss of Varus' three legions in the Teutoburg Forest in AD 9, and the initial conquest campaigns in Britain from the Claudian invasion of AD 43 onwards.
- The Year of the Four Emperors in AD 69, with Vespasian being ultimately successful.
- The Flavian dynasty, from Vespasian's accession to the death of Domitian in AD 96. This included the later campaigns of conquest in Britain and the final destruction of the First Jewish Revolt in AD 70.
- The Nervo-Trajanic dynasty, from the accession of Nerva in AD 96 to the death of Hadrian in AD 138. This included the campaigns of Trajan, including his conquest of Dacia in two campaigns from AD 101–102 and AD 105–106. It also included the destruction of the Second Jewish Revolt in AD 135.
- The Antonine dynasty, from the accession of Antoninus Pius in AD 138 through to the assassination of Commodus in AD 192. The lengthy 23-year reign of Antoninus Pius was one of relative peace, with the empire at its most stable (though much campaigning still took place, for example in Britain).
- The Year of the Five Emperors in AD 193, and the subsequent civil wars. This ranged from the accession of Pertinax through to the death of British governor and usurper Clodius Albinus in AD 197.

- The Severan dynasty, from the accession of Septimius Severus in AD 193 through to the assassination of Severus Alexander in AD 235. This included Severus' two campaigns attempting to conquer Scotland in AD 209 and AD 210.
- The 'crisis of the 3rd century', from the death of Severus Alexander to the accession of Diocletian in AD 284. This period was a time when the empire was under great stress, racked with external conflict and civil war, pestilence in the form of the Plague of Cyprian, and economic depression. All ultimately led to change within and without its borders and the onset of the Dominate period in Roman history. The low point was the capture of Emperor Valerian by the Sassanid Persian King Shapur I at Edessa in AD 260.

Throughout this period the emperor exercised his authority through three main bodies. These were:

- The *consilium principis* main council, created by Augustus as his central advisory body. This was always in session, meeting ad hoc at the emperor's call whenever required to advise on mostly legal and diplomatic matters.
- The *fiscus* imperial treasury, controlled by a *rationibus* financial officer. This was the magnet for the wealth generated in each of the empire's provinces, the territories outside of Italy following the campaigns of conquest in the republic and early empire. The term is very specific, referring to the personal treasury of the emperors of Rome, translating as 'purse' or 'basket'.
- The Praetorian Guard, again founded by Augustus and institutionalised by Tiberius, under the command of Praetorian prefects. This body had a monopoly of force within the walls of Rome through much of the Principate,

then being significantly reformed and expanded by Severus Septimius when emperor. Praetorian guardsmen were often (though not always) elite troops, whose presence so close to the Roman seat of power was often a great source of destabilisation. On campaign they were equipped in a similar manner to the standard legionary.

The emperor was also the supreme commander of every aspect of the Roman military. After the rapid territorial advances of the mid and late republic, by the Principate much of this was forward deployed near the frontiers to enable a rapid, swift and brutal response to any unwanted attention there from *barbaricum*. The legions here were often on the defensive at this time, though exceptions did occur during the reigns of emperors such as Claudius, Trajan and Septimius Severus, who initiated their own campaigns of conquest to further expand the empire.

*Trajan's Column, Rome. Telling the story of this emperor's conquest of Dacia when the Principate legions were at the height of their power.*

# The Dominate Empire

Diocletian was preceded by a number of warrior emperors, for example Aurelian, who began the process of stabilising the empire after the multiple shocks of the 'crisis of the 3rd century.' However, it was he who quickly realised the political structures of the Principate were no longer fit for purpose. From his accession we refer to the Dominate Empire. This referenced a much more authoritarian style of imperial control, with the name itself based on the word *dominus* which references master or lord. Gone was the conceit of the Principate with the emperor the principal citizen of the empire but still 'one of us'. Now, with control of the military and political classes vital to the survival of Rome, he became more akin to an eastern potentate.

Diocletian specifically reformed the empire in three ways:

- Instituting the *tetrarchy* system of political control. This divided power across his vast empire between first two and then four (two senior and two junior) brother-emperors. Note he retained overall control.
- Carrying out the 'Diocletianic reformation' of political organisation across the empire, with *diocese* being created as large economic units of control to replace many of the older provinces. Each *diocese* was then broken down into new, smaller provinces. Under this system the number of older provinces was increased from 47 to nearly 100, each much easier to control given their smaller size.
- Adding extra layers of public administration to support the above, increasing the coercive power of the Roman state. This allowed a fully systemised

taxation regime to be introduced on all economic production called the *annona militaris*. This ensured that taxes rolled in efficiently into the Imperial *fiscus* once more after the economic breakdown of the 'crisis of the 3rd century'.

The principal dynasties were those of Constantine (who completed Diocletian's plan to officially divide the empire into eastern and western halves), Valentinian and Theodosius. The empire in the west finally ended in AD 476 with the deposition of Romulus Augustulus, though was to continue in the east in one form or another until 1453 AD.

Once more, as with the Principate, the emperors of the Dominate Empire were the supreme commanders of the military. They were even more challenged however. Given the inevitable desire of those without the empire to have access to what was within, the borders came under increasing pressure from the mid-2nd century AD. The military changed dramatically in response. Septimius Severus was the first emperor to create a field army, this to invade Scotland in AD 209 and AD 210. This force included his own founding, the legio II Parthica, which was normally based unusually close to Rome, there to put the stamp of his authority on the political classes. This pattern of legions being based away from the borders – in depth as it were, better able to respond to deep strikes within the territory of the empire by ever larger 'barbarian' groups – became more common as the 3rd century AD progressed. It was formalised under Diocletian, and by the time of Constantine (sole emperor from AD 324) the change was striking. By this time the legionaries and other troops of the Principate had been replaced by *comitatenses* field army troops (featuring a much larger proportion of mounted troops than previously) and *limitanei* border troops. The latter acted as a 'trip-wire' force for the former and both are considered in more detail in Chapter 4.

# CHAPTER 2

# THE LEGIONARY

We now turn to the legionaries themselves. In this chapter I consider the origins of the legionary, go into great detail about the life of the Principate legionary, and finally consider the panoply of equipment that – together with his training – made him such an elite warrior.

## The origins of the legionary

We have no real insight into the Roman military tradition until the city came under Etruscan rule. The ensuing Etrusco-Roman army then adopted the Greek-style hoplite phalanx, which the Etruscans had by this time embraced as their principal battle formation after contact with the Greek colonies of southern Italy and eastern Sicily.

Initially, the Etrusco-Roman phalanx was supported on the flanks by Roman/Latin contingents who still fought in an individual manner – just like their Villanovan ancestors – with spears, axes and javelins. This system was formalised by Servius Tullius (see Chapter 1). Under the Servian constitution, Roman society was divided into seven different classes, each of which had a different military commitment to the state. These were based

The term **phalanx** references a deep formation of armoured spearmen. In such a formation the front-rank hoplites fought with their long spears in an overarm thrusting position, covered by the interlocking *hoplon* large round body shield. Those at the rear (up to eight ranks deep) added their weight to the formation, replacing those falling in battle at the front. Warfare using such phalanxes tended to feature the best troops deploying on the right-hand side. This often caused the line of battle to wheel right to left.

on wealth, given the individual warrior had to supply his own military equipment. The seven classes of Roman society were:

- The *equites*, the wealthiest citizens who could afford a mount and thus formed the cavalry.
- The First Class, the next wealthiest forming 80 centuries of hoplite-equipped spearmen fighting as a phalanx. Most of these troops would have been of Etruscan origin.
- The Second Class, 20 centuries of spearmen with helmet, greaves and the *scutum* rectangular shield.
- The Third Class, 20 centuries of spearmen with helmet and *scutum*.
- The Fourth Class, 20 centuries of spearmen with *scutum* only.
- The Fifth Class, 20 centuries of missile troops with slings and javelins.
- The *capite censi,* translating as head count and referencing those in Etrusco-Roman society with little or no property. This class had no military commitment.

Armies formed in this way are often dubbed Tullian Roman. Note *scutum* here refers to an Italian rectangular shield design rather than the much more substantial body shield of the mid-late republic and Principate (see below).

This military system began to evolve after Rome and its fellow Latin towns broke away from Etruscan control. They now faced the hill tribes of the Apennines, such as the Aequi, Umbri, Sabini and Volsci. These fought in a looser formation and often sought battle in rough terrain to negate the power of the First Class phalanx, whose importance began to diminish.

After Rome became a republic with the overthrow of Tarquin the Proud in 509 BC, three key events had a big impact on the development of the Roman military system. The first was the initiation of the eight-year siege of Veii, which ended in 396 BC. The second was the appointment of Marcus Furius Camillus as consular tribune in 401 BC, in the context of the increasingly unpopular siege. The third was the Latin defeat by the Senones Gauls at the battle of Allia in 390 BC, and the subsequent sack of Rome.

These dramatic events led in turn to three developments with the Roman army, together called the Camillan reforms after Camillus. Firstly, in the context of the long siege of Veii, the army began to receive pay for the first time. This was in the form of the *stipendium* cash allowance. Secondly, and crucially, the phalanx was formally abandoned. A key factor here was the height of the Gallic warriors faced at Allia and their fighting technique. They were taller than their Latin counterparts and fought with long iron swords using a downward slashing technique. This rendered the *hoplon*, designed to defend the user and his neighbours from frontal attack, less practical. The final, and connected, development was the abandonment of all previous line-of-battle shields – including the *hoplon* – in favour of the *scutum*. Here the name references the famous specific type rather than the earlier generalised shield.

The outcome of all of these reforms was the appearance of the manipular legion to replace the Tullian Roman system. Initially these were two in number, each commanded by a consul with six *tribuni militum* acting as subordinates. The initial manipular legions numbered 3,000 infantry each, though this quickly increased with time, ultimately numbering over 6,000. Within this legion there were three classes of line-of-battle troops, all termed for the first time legionaries. Based on experience and age rather than the equipment they could afford, these were:

- *triarii*, veterans in helmet and body armour, carrying the *scutum*, *hasta* thrusting spear and sword. These replaced, in part, the old Tullian First Class.
- *principes*, older warriors also in helmet and body armour, carrying the *scutum*, *pila* heavy throwing javelin (of Spanish origin) and sword. The *pila* were used to deliver a devastating volley immediately prior to impact with the opposing battle line. These also replaced, in part, the old Tullian First Class.
- *hastati*, 'the flower of young men', with helmet and lesser body armour, carrying the *scutum*, *pila* heavy throwing javelin and sword. These replaced the old Tullian Second Class.

It is unclear how quickly the *pilum* replaced the spear of the old First and Second Classes for the *principes* and *hastati*, though unusually given they are clearly named after the *hasta* spear, it was the latter who converted to the *pila* first.

All three troop types formed up in a looser formation than the phalanx. This allowed free use of the sword and body shield. The *triarii* could be deployed in closer formation if a hedge of spears was required, for example against cavalry. The legion was completed with three lesser classes of warrior, the *rorarii*, *accensi* and *leves*, who replaced, sequentially, the old Tullian Third, Fourth and Fifth Classes. These troops became less important as the republic progressed.

The manipular legion deployed in three lines. The first comprised 15 maniples of *hastati*, each of around 60 men and two officers. Each of these maniples had 20 *leves* attached to act as skirmishers. The second line then had 15 maniples of *principes*, again each of around 60 men and two officers. The third line comprised 15 *ordines*, each *ordo* comprised of a *vexilla* of *triarii*, a *vexilla* of *rorarii* and a *vexilla* of *accensi*. Each *vexilla* numbered

60 troops and two officers, with the *triarii* additionally featuring a standard bearer.

The *triarii*, as veterans, were the tactical reserve held back to exploit success, plug gaps in the first two lines or to cover a retreat. When not engaged, they deployed kneeling on their right knee. It is less clear how the *rorarii* and *accensi* were utilised, but a deployment on the flanks – as with the older Third and Fourth Tullian classes – or as camp guards seems most likely. This early manipular legion-based army is often called Camillan Roman.

After Rome's conflict with Pyrrhus in the early 3rd century BC the manipular legion further evolved into what historians call the Polybian system. This again deployed in three lines, featuring 1,200 *hastati* in 10 maniples of 120, 1,200 *principes* who were organised in the same way, and 600 *triarii* in 10 maniples of 60. Each maniple featured two centurions, two subordinates and two standard bearers. The major change was the disappearance of the *leves* who were replaced with 1,200 *velites*. These were specialist skirmishers, divided up among the other maniples for administrative purposes. The formal transition from *leves* to *velites* was complete by 211 BC. The *rorarii* and *accensi* also disappear from this point.

The Polybian manipular legion also featured a formal cavalry component. This was 300 strong, divided into 10 *turmae* of 30 troopers. Like the high-status *equites* of the earlier Tullian army, this small force was actually the most prestigious within the legion. However, unlike the later auxiliary cavalry component of the Principate legions that served administrative and scouting functions, these young aristocrats were more likely to charge headlong into battle. Cato for example boasted his grandfather had had five horses killed under him in this manner.

The Polybian legion was highly efficient, and though it struggled against Hannibal in Italy in the later 3rd century BC, was ultimately his nemesis at Zama in 202 BC where its flexibility was the key to a crushing victory. It was also a military system the Hellenistic kingdoms in the eastern Mediterranean never came to terms with, they being repeatedly defeated by it in set-piece battle.

There were four reasons why the manipular legion was so successful:

- Flexibility: the manipular legion was very flexible, deploying in its three lines when opportunity allowed. This ensured the troops in the second and third lines were fresh until needed as the battle progressed, unlike the opposing troops who might all be engaged from first contact (particularly in Hellenistic armies). Further, given the wider spacing of the legionary compared to say the Carthaginian spearman or Macedonian phalangite, more complex manoeuvres could be carried out and rough terrain exploited. The former was key at the battle of Cynoscephalae against Philip V in 197 BC, the latter at the battle of Pydna against Perseus in 168 BC.
- Roman military psyche: in short, reflecting Roman culture more broadly, the manipular legions possessed true grit and were renowned for never giving up. Thus defeat, even if writ large on the battlefield, was never accepted and the Romans kept coming back. This is no more evident than in the context of the Second Punic War (see Chapter 1).
- Adoption of successful tactics and technology: the Roman military was adept at seamlessly assimilating enemy military tactics and technology. Thus Roman naval power had its origins in the First and Second Punic Wars, where the maritime prowess of the Carthaginians provided the template for ultimate Roman naval supremacy. Similarly, as detailed above, the two weapons most associated with the Roman legionary – *gladius and pilum* – were of Spanish origin.
- Loot and plunder: Roman society was heavily structured based on wealth qualifications, especially among the aristocracy. Thus, although Rome was initially hesitant to engage in the western and eastern Mediterranean, the immense wealth of Carthage and the Hellenistic kingdoms ultimately proved an enormous draw. The more successful aristocratic military leaders – in effect warlords with private

armies from the later 2nd and 1st centuries BC – thus made huge fortunes in their campaigns of conquest, with the soldiery equally well motivated through the promise of fabulous plunder.

The principal weapon of the Polybian *principes* and *hastati* – and side arm of the spear-armed *triarii* – was the *gladius Hispaniensis* sword. This was ubiquitous by the mid-3rd century BC. Of Spanish origin, rather than being the short stabbing sword of popular legend it was actually a cut-and-thrust weapon of medium length. The blade, up to 69 cm long and 5 cm in width, featured a tapering sharp stabbing point. It was this weapon that shocked the Macedonians due to the wounds it caused during the Second Macedonian War. Prior to the advent of this weapon, earlier legionaries would have used a leaf-shaped iron blade or curved *kopis*. Whichever weapon was used, unless worn by an officer, it was worn on the right-hand side. Those legionaries who could afford to would also carry a *pugio* 30 cm long dagger.

The Polybian *principes* and *hastati* also carried two *pila* weighted javelins, one heavy and one light. Each had a barbed head on a long, tapering iron shank whose weighted socket, attaching it to the wooden shaft, provided the punching force to hammer the weapon through enemy shields and armour. In terms of specific use, the lighter *pilum* was used as the *principes* and *hastati* approached the enemy. The heavier weapon was then used immediately prior to impact. The long iron shafts were specifically designed to bend after impact and so disable the use of the opponent's shield.

Meanwhile the *triarii* carried the *hasta* long thrusting spear, up to 2.5 metres in length. Harking back to the hoplite origins of the Tullian First Class warrior, this featured a socketed iron spearhead up to 30 cm in length and a bronze butt-spike, the latter acting as a counterweight to the spearhead. The weapon was usually wielded over the right shoulder to deliver a forceful overarm strike, although if used in the charge it could instead be deployed underarm.

In terms of defensive equipment, the basic model of legionary protection for the Polybian *triarii*, *principes* and *hastati* was the *scutum* shield, helmet, armour of some kind for the upper torso and often also the lower legs.

The Polybian *scutum* was a large rectangular curved body shield 120 cm in length and 75 cm in width. It was made from planed wooden strips laminated together in three layers and was very sturdy. An *umbones* iron boss was attached to the centre where the shield was slightly thicker, it being completed with a calf-skin and felt facing. At up to 10 kilograms in weight, it was held by a horizontal grip using a straightened arm. Crucially, rather than just being used for protection, it was also used as an offensive weapon in its own right, being smashed into opponents to push them over.

Legionary helmets were worn by all battle-line troops, no matter their status. Made from bronze at this time, they fitted the cranium and provided good overall protection. Designs called Etrusco-Corinthian, Attic and Montefortino were the most common, and it was usual for such helmets to feature three purple or black feathers standing up to 50 cm in height.

For body armour all legionaries wore a square bronze pectoral 23 cm wide covering the heart and upper chest. This was held in place with leather straps. Older Italic disc-shaped pectorals were also still in use at this time. Those who could afford it, usually *triarii* and *principes,* replaced the primitive pectorals with *lorica hamata* chain mail shirts. Such armour, while offering greatly improved protection, was very heavy at around 15 kg. The shirt, covering the torso from the shoulder to the hips, was of Gallic origin and made from interlinked iron rings 1 mm thick and up to 9 mm in external diameter. Up to 20,000 were needed for each shirt, making its manufacture very labour intensive and expensive.

If the legionary could afford it, his defensive panoply was completed with an iron or bronze greave on the leading left lower leg – both legs for the very well off. This was to prevent a debilitating blow to the shin that would open the legionary's guard to a mortal blow.

The next evolution of the legions was the Marian system of the late republic. It is from this time that we begin to see the legionary as most perceive him today, the ubiquitous warrior of the Principate.

## The Principate legionary

When Marius instituted his reforms he completely reorganised the Roman military. He wanted each legion to be a self-contained fighting force. Therefore, of the 6,000 men in each legion, 4,800 were now a standardised variant of the legionary. This was based on the *gladius-* and *pilum*-armed armed *principes* and *hastati* (though the terms were dropped), with the spear-armed *triarii* and javelin-armed *velites* disappearing entirely. From now on, all fighting men in the legion were simply called legionaries, with the remaining 1,200 men being support staff.

To make his new system work Marius also replaced the old Camillan and Polybian manipular system with centuries commanded by a centurion. Each century comprised 80 legionaries and 20 support staff, sub-divided into units of 10 (eight legionaries and two non-combatants). The troops lived, fought and ate together, with each legion developing their own identity and *esprit de corps*. Marius insisted on regular training and fitness drills, meaning the legionaries were always physically fit.

The training particularly focused on martial skills and was based on the same methods used to train gladiators. For example, for sword drill, a large stake the size of a legionary was set up in the training ground. The trooper then practiced his fencing technique with wooden replica sword and wicker shield, the stake being 'the enemy'. The main focus was to ensure that the legionary thrust his sword rather than slashed, a more difficult blow to anticipate and parry. Meanwhile fitness was essential for the legionary, each man also carrying his own equipment, with the troops earning the nickname *muli mariani* (Marius' mules).

*Principate legionaries supported by a field ballista. (Andy Singleton)*

The main advantage of the new Marian legion was that, as self-contained units, a legion was not reliant on long lines of supply and huge baggage trains. Instead they were very mobile, though one side effect was that it allowed the warlords of the late republic to build private armies of legions to conquer enemy territory (thus gaining vast wealth) and to fight each other. In that context they can be said to have played a crucial part in the downfall of the republic.

The next military reformation was carried out by Augustus, covering every aspect of the armed forces of Rome. This included the legions, their supporting troops (most, from this time, becoming the full-time *auxilia*) and regional fleets. The latter two are considered in more detail in Chapter 4.

Augustus' first move with the legions was to tackle the huge number he had inherited from the recent civil wars, around 60. He reduced this to 28 (this falling to 25 after Varus' losses in Germany in AD 9), and the total would hover around 30 for the next 200 years, for example 29 at the time of the accession of Marcus Aurelius and Lucius Verus in AD 161.

The Principate legions after the Augustan reforms numbered 5,500 men, organised into ten cohorts. Of these, the first had five centuries of 160 men (legio II Parthica's first cohort had six

*The legionary legate, overseeing the deployment of legio II Augusta. (Andy Singleton)*

such centuries), with the other cohorts having six centuries of 80 men. Each normal century was broken down into ten eight-man section – *contubernia* – who shared a tent when on campaign, and two barrack block rooms when in camp. Additionally, the legion also featured 120 auxiliary cavalry acting as dispatch riders and scouts, and support staff.

Principate legionaries could be volunteers or conscripted (under a levy called the *dilectus*), depending on the circumstances, although by the time of Marcus Aurelius they were increasingly enrolled as conscripts. This was usually on a regional basis as with legios II and III Italica. Those recruited (by either means) were exclusively Roman citizens for most of the Principate, originally being all Italian at the end of the republic, although increasingly from Gaul and Spain as citizenship spread. The recruiting base for legionaries then increased dramatically with the Edict of Caracalla in AD 212 as this made every free man living in the empire a citizen. Meanwhile, throughout the Principate and much of the Dominate phases of the empire there was a height requirement for the legionary: 1.8 metres.

The **numbering and naming of the legions** seems confusing to us today, reflecting their being raised by different republican leaders (especially at the time of the civil wars of the late republic) and emperors, and at different times. Therefore many shared the same legion number (always permanent) but had different names, for example there being five third legions. Others shared the same name but with different numbering, for example Septimius Severus' foundings legios I, II and III Parthica. The longevity of this numbering, and the clear differential in the naming, suggests that the strong sense of identity of the Marian legions was carried over into their Augustan counterparts. In that regard, the standards carried by the legions were very important. Each had a variety of types. First and most important was the *aquila* eagle standard carried by the *aquilifer*, the eagle by the time of the Principate made entirely of gold and which only left camp when the entire legion was on the move. Another standard, the *imago*, featured an image of the emperor and was carried by the *imaginifer*, while *signa* standards were allocated to each individual century. These were carried by the *signifer*. Flag-based standards were also used, called *vexilla*, one of which showed the name of the legion, while others of the same type were allocated to legionary detachments, hence their naming as *vexillations*. The *vexilla* were carried by *vexillarii*. They were joined in their signalling role in the legions by the *cornicern* musician who played the *cornu*. The latter always marched at the head of the centuries, with the *signifer* or other appropriate standard bearer.

The Principate legionary term of service was initially 20 years, set by Augustus as part of his military reforms, with the last four as a veteran excused fatigues and guard duty. This length of service was later extended by Augustus to 25 years, with five as a veteran, a term that lasted until the end of the Principate. The increase was due to a shortage of recruits (he being too successful when slimming the number of legions down), and because of the strain placed on the imperial *fiscus* to pay the *praemia* retirement gratuity for retiring legionaries given the very large number of troops Augustus inherited. These gratuities were either of money (3,000 *denarii* in the late 1st century BC, this rising to 5,000 *denarii* by the time of Septimius Severus) or land. In the latter case this was in the form of *centuriated* land parcels or in *colonia* settlements. Such retired legionaries often settled near to their former legionary bases, these settlements then developing into *coloniae* towns as happened with Gloucester (Roman Glevum), Lincoln (Roman Lindum Colonia) and York (Roman Eboracum) in Britain.

In terms of pay the Augustan legionary received 225 *denarii* a year from which deductions were made for arms, clothing and food. This was increased to 300 *denarii* by Domitian (AD 81–96), a level it remained at until the reign of Septimius Severus who increased it to 450 *denarii*. His son Caracalla increased legionary pay even more, by a further 50 per cent, following his father's advice to keep the soldiery happy above all else. This basic pay was often increased through donatives such as the 75 *denarii* left by Augustus to all of his legionaries in his will. Even at its most basic level this was a good salary for a Roman citizen, and in an age before popular banking the legionaries often handed their savings to their unit standard bearers, a duty that placed a huge amount of trust upon them. To provide some context here as to the impact this all had on the imperial *fiscus*, in the 2nd century AD the overall cost of the military was 150 million *denarii* (comprising salaries and retirement gratuities).

Like all armies, the legions marched on their stomachs. In that regard, Vegetius in his late 4th-century AD military manual says that troops should never be without corn, wine, vinegar and salt. This

*Caracalla, styled on the arch of his father Septimius Severus, with a captive Parthian during their eastern campaigns.*

was the same for Roman troops of all periods, with bread, beans, porridge, eggs and vegetables forming the core diet of the legionary. Meat would be eaten on feast days, the wider diet then being supplemented by local produce and hunting. When on campaign, the daily staples were hard tack and whole-wheat biscuits, together with bread baked at the end of the day's march after the marching camp had been built. Great care was taken on such campaigns to ensure the security of the supply of grain to the legions. This is well evidenced by the Scottish campaigns of Septimius Severus in Scotland where he expanded the size of the granaries at the key supply base at South Shields (Roman *Arbeia*) by a factor of 10.

Religion was a key element in the daily lives experienced by the legionaries of the Principate, playing a major role in their appreciation of belief and belonging. Given the legionary was a citizen of Rome he was clearly obliged to honour the gods of the Roman pantheon, in particular Jupiter, Juno and Minerva given their association with the empire's capital. To these in terms of popularity one can of course also add Mars given his obvious association as the god of war, while worship of gods associated with the location of a given legion's place or origin (often a local deity assimilated into the Roman pantheon) was also common. Additionally, certain gods also had a specific association with the military. These included the eastern deity Mithras who was popular with Roman soldiery across the empire. Worship of these gods, and also the dates of the traditional festivals of Rome (together with the accession days and birthdays of emperors), structured the religious year for the legionary.

Elsewhere in the legionary's daily life, they were officially unable to marry until retirement, though they often contracted technically illegal marriages. This was changed by Septimius Severus who granted the soldiers the right to marry, and gave illegal spouses and offspring legal rights for the first time.

In terms of command structure, the legions from the early Principate were led by a senatorial-level *legatus legionis*. His second-in-command was also of senatorial-level, called the *tribunus laticlavius*, a younger man gaining the experience needed to command their own legion in the future. Third in command was the *praefectus castrorum* (camp prefect), a seasoned former centurion responsible for administration and logistics. Below this level there were five younger equestrian-level tribunes, called the *tribuni angusticlavii*, these allocated tasks and responsibilities as necessary.

The actual control of each cohort in the legion was the responsibility of the centurions (six to a normal cohort), they having specific titles reflecting their seniority based on the old manipular legions of the Camillan and Polybian periods. These names, their seniority in ascending order, were: *hastatus posterior, hastatus prior, princeps posterior, princeps prior, pilus posterior* and *pilus prior.*

# Equipment of the Principate legionary

Principate Roman legionaries were for the most part specialist heavy infantry whose arms and armour were always geared towards defeating their opponents through the shock of impact and discipline (although see below regarding legionary *lanciarii*). This was a direct continuation of the role of the Camillan and Polybian *principes* and *hastati*, and Marian legionary.

The principal weapon was still the *gladius*, as before worn on the right-hand side for rank-and-file troopers. When Augustus took office the main type was still the *gladius Hispaniensis*. This developed during his reign into the Mainz-type *gladius* that was broader and shorter, featuring a longer stabbing point. A further development, adopted towards the close of the 1st century AD, was the Pompeii-type *gladius*, this being slightly shorter than Mainz type with a shorter, triangular stabbing point. All of these weapons still used the same cut-and-thrust combat technique, which continued to dominate Roman fencing techniques even when the length of the swords began to increase again in the later 2nd century AD.

The Principate legionary also still carried his two *pilum* weighted javelins, again one light for use in the approach and one heavy for use immediately prior to impact.

The weapons complement was completed by the *pugio* dagger. Both this and the *gladius* were suspended from two individual belts that crossed over front and back.

For a shield the Principate legionary was still equipped with the curved, rectangular *scutum* (though squarer in design than those of their republican counterparts). As before it was used as an offensive weapon in its own right, and in defence allowed the legionaries to adopt a number of defensive formations including the *testudo*. This featured interlocking shields providing full cover on all sides, including from above.

In terms of armour the legionaries of the Principate wore a variety of types of full body armour. The most commonly depicted in contemporary culture and found in the archaeological record is the famous *lorica segmentata*, constructed of articulated iron plates and hoops. As time progressed, this complicated though highly effective armour was simplified for ease of use by the legionary, one example found at the *principia* (headquarters building) at the *vexillation* fortress of Newsteads (Roman *Trimontium*) in 1905 featuring simple rivets to replace earlier bronze hinges, a single large girdle plate replacing the two previous ones and strong hooks replacing earlier and more complicated belt-buckle fastenings. Simplification of this armour continued through to its demise.

Other types were also worn, some with their roots in the republic such as the *lorica hamata* long chain mail shirt. This continued in use throughout the Principate and came back into full favour in the 3rd century AD (see below). A further variant was *lorica squamata* scale mail (cheaper than chain mail but inferior in flexibility and protection), while in the provinces even more exotic types were to be found, for example a suit of crocodile-skin armour found in a 3rd-century AD context in Manfalut, Egypt, and now housed in the British Museum. It is not clear in such cases if the function of the armour was more religious than military, in this instance perhaps with a military crocodile cult.

Additionally, when fighting certain types of opponent (such as Dacians using the two-handed *falx* slashing weapon) extra armour was fitted including articulated iron *manicae* arm guards, thigh guards and greaves. Specific troop types within the legions were also often differentially equipped with armour when compared to the rank-and-file legionaries to mark them apart, with officers frequently shown wearing iron and bronze muscled cuirasses and centurions and *signifers* wearing chain mail (even when the majority of legionaries were wearing *lorica segmentata*).

Finally in terms of military equipment, the helmet of the legionary also evolved throughout the Principate. The traditional republican Montefortino type was still in use when Augustus became emperor, though the mid-republican Etrusco-Corinthian and Attic types had disappeared by then. However two new types had appeared in the generation before Augustus, reflecting a Celtic influence following Caesar's campaigns in Gaul. These were the Coolus type with a round cap of bronze and small neck guard (which disappeared in the middle of the

1st century AD), and iron Port type with a deep neck guard, the latter named after the site type location of Port bei Nidau in Switzerland. This latter developed into the classic 'imperial' Gallic helmet often associated with the Roman legionary of the 1st and 2nd centuries AD, featuring an even larger neck guard. A final 'imperial' type was that originating in Italy, hence it being called Italic, a bronze compromise between the new designs of Celtic origin and the more traditional Roman types. All of these helmets featured prominent cheek guards (again of Celtic provenance) and often a reinforcing strip on the front of the cap to deflect downward sword slashes. Ear guards had been added by the AD 50s.

This traditional Principate legionary panoply was beginning to change by the late 2nd/early 3rd centuries AD. This was largely a response to a change in the nature of their opponents. Previously, the legions had most often faced a similar infantry-heavy force (excepting the Parthians in the east), but were now tackling a multitude of threats, many of a differing nature that required a more flexible response. This change is shown in real time on three of the monuments set up in Rome by three great warrior

*Arch of Septimius Severus in the Forum, Rome. Built by the warrior emperor on the doorstep of the curia Senate House to demonstrate his power to the elite of Rome.*

emperors – the column of Marcus Aurelius and the arches of Septimius Severus and Constantine.

First, from the reign of Septimius Severus a great change began with the sword, the longer cavalry-style *spatha* beginning to replace the shorter *gladius* for all Roman foot soldiers. This was up to 80 cm in length, although some of one metre in length have been identified. The new sword was suspended from a baldric on a Sarmatian-type scabbard slide, and came to dominate Roman military equipment in the West until the empire's end there, continuing in use the East afterwards. It seems likely the adoption of this weapon had its origins in a need for more reach to tackle armoured mounted opponents.

A similar change is also evident in the use of the *pila*, they gradually being replaced by a thrusting spear of between 2 metres and 2.7 metres in length over the same time period. This change is visible actually taking place on the three monuments detailed above. Thus on the Column of Marcus Aurelius legionaries in classic *lorica segmentata* armour (of banded iron, see below) are mostly armed with *pila*, while on the Arches of Severus and Constantine they have been replaced by spears. This was almost certainly a response to the experiences in fighting mounted opponents more frequently, as with the longer sword. In this regard, Rome had long engaged with Parthian heavy shock cavalry and supporting horse archers in the east, but in the Marcommanic Wars under Marcus Aurelius and Lucius Verus they also found themselves fighting against the Iazyges Sarmatian tribe who had a much higher proportion of mounted shock troops. A legionary spear wall would therefore have made much more sense engaging such opponents than the use of *pilum* impact weapons.

This change is also evident with the shield. As the 2nd century AD progressed the traditional *scutum* began being replaced by a large flat (and sometimes slightly dished) oval shield, confusingly still called a *scutum*. This new design was of simple plank construction, with stitched-on rawhide, and was strengthened with iron bars. The two types appear to have been used side by side for some time, with examples of both found

*Detail of mid-2nd century AD legionaries in* lorica segmentata *and* auxilia *in mail shirts. Re-used panels from a demolished Arch of Antoninus Pius in Rome found on the much later Arch of Constantine.*

at the fortified frontier trading town of Dura-Europos in Syria dating to AD 256. This transition is also very evident on the three monuments detailed above, with many of the large round shields featuring on the Severan arch, and even more on the Arch of Constantine. Once again this change seems associated with the type of opponent more commonly being faced, the round shield perhaps more suited to dealing with a mounted threat. The new shield certainly gave greater freedom of movement, allowing the legionaries with their new swords and spears to make use of their longer reach, and would also have been cheaper to produce.

Not surprisingly, a change is also evident in the body armour of the legionary as the Principate approached its end. Thus on the Column of Marcus Aurelius most are wearing *lorica segmentata*, while on the Arch of Septimius Severus there is a much higher proportion wearing *lorica hamata* and *lorica squamata*, this proportion increasing yet again the Arch of Constantine.

Meanwhile, as the Principate progressed, legionary helmets also became increasingly substantial, with the Italic 'Imperial' type disappearing in the early 3rd century AD. By this time many legionaries were being equipped with heavier, single bowl designs reinforced by cross-pieces and fitted with deep napes, leaving only a minimal T-shaped face opening. These provided exceptional levels of protection.

A final change in this time period was the appearance of a new type of legionary. This was the *lanciarii* light trooper armed with a quiver of javelins and lighter armour than their front rank line-of-battle equivalents. Such troops, who operated like the *velites* of the Polybian legions, skirmished forward to deter mounted bowmen and other lightly armed missile troops. They are first attested in gravestone epigraphy in the ranks of legio II Parthica in the context of Caracalla and Macrinus' Parthian War, AD 215–218.

For non-military kit, when on the march all legionaries carried non-essential equipment on a T-shaped pole resting on his shoulders, with his shield held in place on his back. Helmets were normally strung from the neck across the front of the chest. The marching kit itself would normally have included a *paenula* hooded woollen bad weather cloak made from thick wool, this fastening with toggles or a button on the centre of the chest. Officers would have worn the shorter rectangular *sagum* that fastened on the right shoulder using a brooch. Meanwhile, a very important piece of kit for the legionary were his hobnailed *caligae* sandals, especially given the huge distance the soldier was expected to march during his military career. A typical piece of legionary footwear featured a leather upper made from single leather pieces sewn at the heel, these stitched to a multiple-layer hide sole that was shod with many iron studs. Each sandal could weigh up to 1 kg. The legionary would also carry a sturdy cross-braced satchel for his personal effects, a *patera* bronze mess tin, a water skin in a net bag, a cooking pot and canvas bags for grain rations, spare clothing, and bespoke engineering equipment (see Chapter 4). Altogether this meant the overall marching load of the average legionary was an impressive 30 kg, Marian mules indeed.

## The Principate legions

| Legion | When founded | Destroyed/ disbanded |
|---|---|---|
| legio I Germanica | Later republic | Disbanded AD 70 after Civilis Revolt |
| legio I Adiutrix pia fidelis | Provisionally recruited by Nero, then made a regular legion by Galba. | |
| legio I Italica | Under Nero | |
| legio I Macriana | Under Nero | Civil war legion, disbanded AD 69/70 |
| legio I Flavia Minervia pia fidelis | Under Domitian | |
| legio I Parthica | Under Septimius Severus | |
| legio II Augusta | Later republic/under Augustus | |
| legio II Adiutrix pia fidelis | Under Nero | |
| legio II Italica | Under Marcus Aurelius | |
| legio II Parthica | Under Septimius Severus | |
| legio II Traiana fortis | Under Trajan | |
| legio III Augusta pia fidelis | Later republic/under Augustus | |
| legio III Cyrenaica | Later republic | |
| legio III Gallica | Under Caesar | |
| legio III Italica concors | Under Marcus Aurelius | |
| legio III Parthica | Under Septimius Severus | |
| legio IIII Flavia felix | Under Vespasian | |
| legio IIII Macedonica | Under Caesar | Disbanded AD 70 |
| legio IIII Scythica | Under Mark Antony | |

| Legion | When founded | Destroyed/ disbanded |
|---|---|---|
| legio V Alaudae | Under Caesar | Destroyed under Domitian |
| legio V Macedonica | Later republic | |
| legio VI Ferrata fidelis constans | Under Caesar | |
| legio VI Victrix | Later republic | |
| legio VII Claudia pia fidelis | Under Caesar | |
| legio VII Gemina | Under Galba | |
| legio VIII Augusta | Later republic | |
| legio IX Hispana | Later republic | Possibly destroyed in the reign of Hadrian during the Bar Kochba rebellion in Judea |
| legio X Fretensis | Later republic | |
| legio X Gemina | Under Caesar | |
| legio XI Claudia pia fidelis | Later republic | |
| legio XII Fulminata | Under Caesar | |
| legio XIII Gemina pia fidelis | Later republic | |
| legio XIV Gemina Martia Victrix | Later republic | |
| legio XV Apollinaris | Under Augustus | |
| legio XV Primigenia | Under Caligula | Disbanded AD 70 |
| legio XVI Flavia Firma | Under Vespasian | |
| legio XVI Gallica | Under Augustus | Disbanded AD 70 |
| legio XVII | Under Augustus | Destroyed in AD 9 in Germany |
| legio XVIII | Under Augustus | Destroyed in AD 9 in Germany |
| legio XIX | Under Augustus | Destroyed in AD 9 in Germany |
| legio XX Valeria Victrix | Under Augustus | |
| legio XXI Rapax | Under Augustus | Possibly destroyed under Domitian |
| legio XXII Deiotariana | Under Augustus | Possibly destroyed under Hadrian |
| legio XXII Primigenia pia fidelis | Under Caligula | |
| legio XXX Ulpia Victrix | Under Trajan | |

After A. Goldsworthy, *The Complete Roman Army*. London: Thames and Hudson, 2003.

# CHAPTER 3

# ON CAMPAIGN AND IN BATTLE

Having detailed the origins, life experiences and equipment of the Principate legionary, I now turn to the activities of these elite warriors on campaign and in battle.

## On campaign

The Roman legions of the Principate were dynamic, flexible and highly efficient, in the most brutal sense. Well organised and motivated, they won their campaign objectives through the total subjugation of their opponents. Even in loss, they most often returned to hammer away until final victory. Varus' loss of three legions in the Teutoburg Forest in AD 9 is the only notable exception during the Principate, when Augustus refused to re-form legio XVII, legio XVIII and legio XIX after they lost their *aquila* eagle standards to Arminius' Germans. Even in Scotland, the darkest corner on the north west border of the empire, Rome kept returning, never satisfied that the far north of the province of Britannia remained elusive. The secret to the success of the legions on campaign was twofold:

- Dynamism: The legions as envisaged by Marius during his reforms (and later by Augustus) were to be autonomous

*Supplying the army in the field. Roman military leaders always paid close attention to logistics. (Andy Singleton)*

formations able to operate alone or in groups in enemy territory. As such, they formed legionary spearheads that powered through the battle space, always keeping the enemy on the back foot until victory was achieved. The main objective here, more often than not, was to force a meeting engagement in the form of a major battle. A decisive victory would then be followed by a swift peace, on terms always agreeable to Rome.

- Logistics: The Romans were masters at ensuring a secure supply chain for their legions when on campaign, making maximum use of marine transport when necessary (both along the coast and up river systems).

To illustrate the nature of this successful campaigning strategy, of which the legions and their legionaries were the focal point, I use three examples. The first features Julius Caesar immediately prior to the Principate and his 55 BC and 54 BC incursions into Britain, and his later siege of Alesia. The latter completed his conquest of

Gaul. Together these show the value placed by the Romans and legionaries on combined arms operations and siege warfare. Next, I turn to the 1st century AD initial campaign of conquest in Britain by Claudius in AD 43, which succeeded where Caesar arguably failed. Finally, I consider the campaigns of Septimius Severus to conquer Scotland, these showing how the Romans were able to gather and keep an enormous force of legionaries and other troops in the field, and in the most difficult of conditions.

*Detail on the Arch of Septimius Severus in the Forum, Rome, showing Roman legionaries engaging Parthian cataphracts.*

*Detail on the Arch of Septimius Severus in the Forum, Rome, showing his eastern campaigns against the Parthians and others in the later AD 190s.*

Before the reforms of Britain by the Severan dynasty in the early 3rd century AD the term **Britannia** references the original single province of Britannia. This was founded after the AD 43 Claudian invasion. After their reforms it references either Britannia Superior or Britannia Inferior, depending on the context (sometimes both). Moving on, in the later 3rd century AD the Diocletianic reformation established the *diocese* of Britannia. This featured no fewer than four provinces, called Maxima Caesariensis, Flavia Caesariensis, Britannia Prima and Britannia Secunda. A fifth province in the *diocese* called Valentia is detailed in the later 4th century AD, though its existence is problematic.

## Caesar in Britain and Gaul

Caesar's landings in Britain were in effect large-scale armed reconnaissances and show the legions of the late republic in close detail. They took place as his campaigns to conquer Gaul were almost complete. He was keenly aware of the support being given to remaining Gallic resistance from Britain, and knew it was here that the Gallic elites who refused to bow to the might of Rome were fleeing. He therefore decided to act, and decisively.

For his first attempt in 55 BC Caesar marched his legionaries from legio VII and legio X (around 12,000 men) north to the territory of the Morini opposite Kent. Here he gathered 80 transports and 18 additional vessels modified to carry horses, together with war galleys from the Mediterranean. Knowing the value of scouting, he then sent his tribune Caius Volusenus in a *trireme* to identify a safe landing area on the east Kent coast. Caesar then waited for favourable conditions before crossing the Channel, arriving in late August off Dover, though his cavalry transports missed the tide and never arrived. Here he found native British troops massed on the coast awaiting his arrival, no doubt bolstered by Gallic refugees, and so he headed north. His fleet eventually weighed anchor between Walmer and Pegwell Bay, below Ramsgate. However, the Britons had tracked his fleet and were once again arrayed along the shore. He therefore carried out an amphibious assault, with the fleet and the legions working closely together. War galleys were driven hard ashore to the north of Caesar's chosen landing area, the aim being to turn the Britons' right flank. From this position the *quinqeremes*, *quadiremes* and *triremes* (five, four and three banks of oars respectively) were able to enfilade the landing area using ballista (firing bolts and large stones) and hand-held missile weapons. However, even then the legionaries were reluctant to land as the Britons held their ground. An incident now occurred that shows the importance of the sense of identity and honour within the legions. This was when the *aquilifer* of legio X, sensing the reticence of his colleagues to disembark, leapt into the shallows and declared 'Leap, fellow soldiers, unless you wish to betray your eagle to the enemy. I, for my part, will perform my duty to the republic and to my general.' This worked, the shamed legionaries swarming ashore, even though the larger transports struggled to get close to the beach as their design proved unsuitable for northern waters. A ferrying operation therefore seems likely from the transports to smaller ships. Once engaged in hand-to-hand combat the legionaries were quickly successful and the defeated leaders of the Britons sued for peace. However, bad weather later damaged many of Caesar's ships and, after some regional campaigning, the Romans returned to the Continent using the remaining serviceable ships.

Our best insight into this initial campaign comes in the form of marching camps. These were one of the best examples of the engineering prowess of the legionary (see Chapter 4). Marching camps were large-scale temporary fortifications built by the legionaries at the end of a day's march in enemy territory, and were an essential feature of the Roman military experience. They were constructed in a few hours and came in a variety of sizes dependent on the scale of the force that needed protection. Almost always rectangular in shape, they generally featured a deep ditch 1–2 metres wide, with the spoil then being used to create an internal rampart. Atop this ran a palisade created by the stakes the troops carried as part of their specialist engineering equipment, either a continuous wooden barrier or one created by the stakes being lashed together to form large caltrops. Within this barrier the camp would then be set out for the night, effectively recreating the interior layout of a permanent Roman fortification. When it was time to move on, the camp was struck in swift order. This was done in a very specific way, with the first trumpet call from the *cornicern* signalling the legionaries to strike their tents, the second telling them to ready the pack animals and destroy the camp, and the third to fall into marching ranks.

Even though the camps were deliberately slighted to deny their use to any enemy after being abandoned, their substantial nature means that today archaeologists can track the path of a Roman campaign in enemy territory by tracing the ditches, banks and crop marks left behind. Some of the best examples from across the empire are to be found in Britain, especially in Wales and Scotland. However, until recently Caesar's campaigns in Britain proved problematic as there were no recorded marching camps in Kent or the south-east. This has recently been addressed though, through the remarkable finding of a 20-hectare marching camp at Pegwell Bay. Here, archaeologists have uncovered a defensive ditched enclosure similar to those found in Caesar's later siege of Alesia in Gaul, in which was found a *pilum* head and mid-1st century BC pottery. They have interpreted this as being evidence of Caesar's first incursion. The find is particularly significant as it shows Caesar's intention was not simply to raid ashore with his troops during the day and then return to the vessels of his fleet for the night, but his plans were far more significant, involving intense campaigning on land.

Showing typical Roman grit, Caesar determined the next year to return once more, and in much greater force. Thus in 54 BC he gathered five legions and 2,000 cavalry. Learning from his experiences the previous year regarding the type of vessel best suited for amphibious operations in Britain, he also ordered the construction of 600 specially built ships. These featured lower freeboards than his Mediterranean designs to enable easier disembarkation, and wider beams to carry bulkier loads. To these vessels Caesar added 200 locally chartered transports, a further 80 ships that had survived the previous year's incursion, and 28 war galleys (again a mix of *quinqeremes*, *quadiremes* and *triremes* from the Mediterranean).

The size of Caesar's force clearly intimidated the Britons as the landing on the east coast of Kent was this time unopposed. Just as in 55 BC however, bad weather intervened again. While Caesar was campaigning inland against a large British force that had eventually gathered to confront him, a storm badly damaged many of his transports anchored off the coast of Kent. Realising the vulnerability to his rear he quickly returned to the landing area and initiated an urgent repair operation (with many of the vessels being dragged onto the beach to prevent further damage in the bad weather). The legions then renewed their campaign against the Britons, with the spearheads of legionaries forcing a crossing of the Thames (supported by his war galleys, again showing combined arms in action) and capturing the main base of the British leader Cassivellaunus who then sued for peace. Honour satisfied, Caesar returned to the landing area in Kent and re-embarked his forces for the return journey to north-east Gaul, this taking place in two waves given the scale of ship losses in the earlier storm. The first wave travelled to the continent safely, but the vessels were prevented from returning by more bad weather. Caesar then deciding to risk cramming his remaining troops into the few serviceable vessels left in Britain, almost certainly the war galleys. These arrived safely back at the end of September. Thus ended his engagements with Britain.

By 52 BC Caesar's conquest of Gaul was almost complete. However, many of the Gallic tribes remained rebellious. They found a new leader in Vercingetorix of the Averni tribe, around whom resistance coalesced. A mass revolt followed, prompting Caesar to target the Averni capital Gergovia with typical speed. Though repulsed, Roman grit showed through again, the legions fighting a prolonged campaign that forced Vercingetorix and 60,000 of his men to take shelter in the fortified hilltop town of Alesia. Here Caesar determined to starve Vercingetorix into surrender, and we see Roman siege warfare at its best. He ordered his men to construct ditches and an earthen bank topped by a palisade, just as with the marching camps but far grander in scale, an astonishing 18 kilometres long. This wall was interspersed with timber towers, enabling legionaries and archers to enfilade any attackers to the front or rear. The whole enclosed the town in a *circumvallation*. We have great insight here into the sophistication of this fortification thanks to Caesar's detailed description. The bank and palisade was 3.6 metres high, with sharpened forked branches projecting outwards towards Alesia. Beyond this, two ditches were dug, each 4.4 metres wide and 2.4 metres deep. The one nearest the bank and palisade featured an 'ankle breaker' in the bottom, a step cut into its base designed to trap the feet of those scrambling to get up the other side and snap ankle bones if due care wasn't taken. The ditch further out was filled with water wherever possible, requiring the Roman engineers to line it with clay. Further out from the bank and palisade another, shallower trench 1.5 metres deep was dug into which were placed five rows of sharpened stakes. Beyond these was a formation of pits up to 1 metre wide in repeating *quincunx* formation (four in the corners of a square and one in the centre) featuring more stakes, this time concealed. These were nicknamed lilies. Finally, even further out, there was a band of *stimuli*, wooden blocks embedded in the ground into which iron barbs had been placed.

The Gauls responded with constant raids against the building works, but failed to slow progress. Then, as construction neared completion, a large force of Gallic cavalry burst through and made off. Caesar, guessing they had been sent to fetch assistance, began a second ditch, bank and palisade fortification to the rear of the first, matching the one facing Alesia. At 22 kilometres long

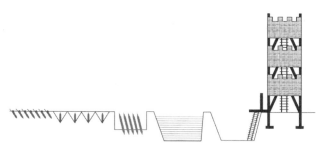

*Cross-section of Roman siege lines at Alesia showing, left to right: stimuli, lilies in quincunx formation, five rows of sharpened stakes, ditch with water, ditch with ankle breaker and finally a wooden tower. (Paul Baker)*

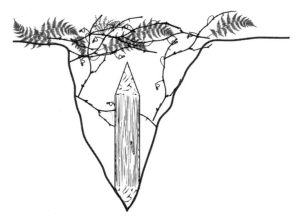

*A 'lilly'. (Paul Baker)*

*A 'stimuli'. (Paul Baker)*

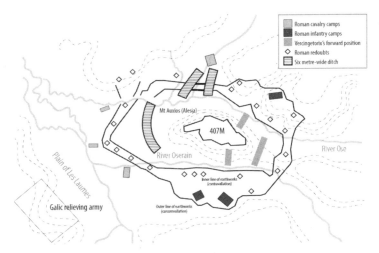

*The Roman siege lines at Alesia. (Paul Baker)*

this wall was even grander, facing outward to cover his rear and forming a *contravallation*. There was only one area of weakness in this outer wall, a section where large boulders and a deep ravine made it impossible to build a continuous fortification. Caesar decided to mask the spot with a kink in the wall.

An incident next occurred that showed the Romans at their most brutal and determined. Vercingetorix, to save whatever food remained for his warriors, forced all of the women and children out of the gates of Alesia. He hoped the Romans would let them pass through Roman lines. However Caesar refused and they had no choice but to camp between the town and the fortifications where they slowly starved.

In late September a Gallic relief army arrived. It quickly launched an attack on the *contravallation* outer wall. Vercingetorix then also attacked from Alesia against the *circumvallation* inner wall. The legionaries fought off both attacks, but the assaults were renewed the following night and continued over the next few days. The Roman besiegers thus found themselves the besieged, between their two siege lines. Then, on 2 October, the Gauls attacked the weak spot in the Roman outer wall, with Vercingetorix again coordinating his assault against the inner wall. Caesar quickly realised the attack would be difficult to defend and poured in reinforcements, while distracting Vercingetorix against the inner wall by sallying legionaries out into the open. Despite valiant efforts in both areas Caesar now saw both of his lines were in danger of breaking. To save the day he personally led 6,000 cavalry from the outer walls. These rode to the rear of the Gauls there, attacking them as they assaulted the palisade. The Gauls were butchered, the survivors breaking and routing. The Roman cavalry pursued them closely, causing more slaughter, eventually overrunning the Gallic camp.

Vercingetorix now knew he was defeated and began negotiating with Caesar who agreed to spare the lives of his men, though the Gallic leader was sent to Rome in chains. It was to be a dramatic fall from grace, the one-time king held captive for five years before forming the centrepiece of Caesar's triumphal parade after which he was executed by strangulation. Such was the lot of those who opposed Rome and the legionaries.

## The Claudian invasion of Britain

While Caesar can be credited with the first and second Roman invasions of Britain, it was the third that successfully set up the province of Britannia, changing the history of the islands forever. This was that of Claudius in AD 43, which showed the legionaries at their most resilient as they campaigned in the almost mythical land, across *oceanus* (as the Romans styled the seas outside of the Mediterranean) and far from their Mediterranean homes.

The Claudian invasion had its origins in the earlier and farcical attempt by Caligula to mount an expedition to conquer Britain in AD 40. For this cancelled operation detailed planning had taken place, including the building at Boulogne of a lighthouse, extensive harbour works, wharfing, fully stocked warehouses and 900 ships. These were all still in place when the ill-favoured Claudius turned his attention to Britain in AD 43, determined to make his name through conquest.

Opportunity was provided by the death of Cunobelinus, king of the Catuvellauni, whose territory covered much of the south-east north of modern London. He was succeeded by Caratacus and Togodumnus, his two sons, who launched an offensive against their Atrebates neighbours – allies of Rome – in the Thames Valley. The Catuvellauni were victorious, with the Atrebatian king Verica fleeing to Rome. Here he sought an audience with Claudius. Caratacus and Togodumnus now overplayed their hand, demanding Verica's extradition. Claudius rebuffed them, with disturbances following in Britain against Roman merchants already embedded in the future Province. With the means already available thanks to Caligula, and now the opportunity, Claudius decided to invade. The scene was set for one of the greatest amphibious operations in the pre-modern world.

Claudius took no chances. He gathered his army of conquest under the highly experienced Pannonian Governor Aulus Plautius, with another seasoned warrior in the future Emperor Vespasian appointed as one of the legionary legates. The invasion force comprised four legions (legio II Augusta, legio IX Hispana, legio XIV Gemina and legio XX Valeria Victrix) together with auxiliaries, totalling 40,000 men. The 900 ships were also loaded with 3,000 tonnes of grain, sufficient to feed the invasion force for at least three months.

A controversy now occurred. The legionaries, superstitious of *oceanus* and mysterious Britain, refused to board their ships. At the last minute the day was saved by one of Claudius' own freedmen, Narcissus, who boarded a vessel and shamed the soldiery into following him. The huge force then set sail in three divisions, arriving unopposed in mid to late summer, when the British warriors had dispersed to gather the harvest. The landing place was again on the east Kent coast. Once ashore Plautius secured his beachhead by building a huge 57-hectare marching camp, the remains of which can still be seen today at the site of the later Saxon Shore fort of Richborough. Some 640 metres of the defensive ditch have been revealed to date. The sophistication of this fortification is indicated by the presence of a gate tower found by archaeologists on the western side.

Plautius now began his breakout, his 40,000 men snaking along the south side of the North Downs where he could expect the most sunlight during the day. This was also the most fertile and heavily populated part of Late Iron Age (LIA) Kent, with the newly gathered harvest available to plunder. His huge column featured the baggage train in the centre, with the legionaries and *auxilia* on the flanks, front and rear. Meanwhile his cavalry *ala* scouted ahead, ranging far and wide, ensuring there were no ambushes and raiding local settlements whenever the opportunity presented itself.

Finally he tracked down his elusive foe, defeating Caratacus and Togodumnus separately in two small engagements in eastern Kent, after which the Dobunni (a tribe based in the Welsh Marches who supplied troops to support the Catuvellauni) became the first of the British kingdoms to sue for peace. Plautius then continued his advance, arriving on the eastern bank of the River Medway at Alyesford where he found a much larger force of Britons on the far shore ready to block his advance. This was the lowest fordable point on the river and here he fought the 'river crossing battle' referenced by the primary sources. A close-run thing it was too.

This battle is interesting in that as it shows the legionaries were often not able to secure victory on their own, relying (as detailed in Chapter 5) on other troop types for support when required. At first Plautius tried to force the ford, but his legionaries were repulsed with heavy losses, despite pouring volleys of *pila* into the Britons and closing with *scutum* and *gladius*. Repeated attempts were made but failed, and at the end of the day he withdrew his troops to build a marching camp. British chariots and cavalry pursued them the whole way.

Plautius knew a change of plan was needed and came up with a clever stratagem to turn the flank of the Britons the following day. In the ranks of his auxiliaries he had some native Batavians from the Rhine Delta, famous for being able to swim in full armour.

Before dawn he ordered these to cross the Medway north of the battle site using inflated pigskins as floats. Once on the western bank they marched upriver and attacked the British chariot and cavalry horses in their corrals in a surprise assault. Then, with panic spreading through the British ranks, Plautius ordered his legionaries forward yet again to force a river crossing. This time they were triumphant and the Britons broke, the survivors bolting north along the Medway, heading for the River Thames. This they reached near modern Higham, crossing over into Essex near modern East Tilbury, making use of islands and marshes in the river. The Britons then drew up on the north bank to contest any crossing of the Thames, given the Catuvellauni capital of Camulodunum (modern Colchester) was only 60 kilometres to the north.

Plautius was hot on their heels, his *ala* of cavalry maintaining contact. In short order he too was on the Thames and once more deployed his troops to force a river crossing. He had learned from the first crossing battle though, and determined to make good use of all of the forces at his disposal. First, he deployed the legionaries immediately opposite the Britons to pin them in place. Next, he used the war galleys and transports for the first time on campaign – the Medway crossing battle had been above the tidal reach of that river, with his ships unable to help there. In the first instance he used the ships to ferry *auxilia* to the north bank of the Thames, downriver of the Britons. He then used his engineers (see Chapter 4) to build a bridge of boats upriver of the Britons. Legionaries from one of the legions then quickly crossed over there. Finally, with legionaries to the west of the Britons and *auxilia* to the east, Plautius launched the assault with his main force directly across the river. Supported by ballista and missile-armed marines on his war galleys, victory was swift and brutal, the broken Britons again fleeing north, this time for their capital. The Romans once more pursued vigorously, though the primary sources say that many of the fleeing Britons used their knowledge of the local marshy terrain to make good their escape. In their eagerness many of the pursuing Romans got into difficulty, some being ambushed and killed.

*Large Roman siege ballista from the Principate with legionary specialists wearing* lorica segmentata *and* lorica hamata. *(Andy Singleton)*

Plautius now paused and consolidated his position, having learned that Togodumnus was dead and Caratacus had fled to the west to find sanctuary with the Silures and Ordovices tribes in Wales. He was weary of over-extending his lines of supply and so built another huge marching camp before re-supplying his army using the fleet. At the same time he sent for Claudius to join him to share the final victory. The emperor, waiting near Boulogne, crossed the Channel quickly and arrived at Plautius' camp with war elephants and camels to intimidate the native Britons. The force then broke camp and headed north at speed for Camulodunum, arriving in late October. The lightning strike smashed all before it and the Catuvellauni quickly sued for peace, eleven other British tribes also submitting to Roman rule. Claudius then declared the province of Britain founded, established Camulodunum as its capital and appointed Plautius its first governor. He then left, never to return, having stayed just 16 days.

This campaign is illustrative for a number of reasons in the context of the legionary on campaign. Firstly, given Caesar's evident failures in the 1st century BC and the known jeopardy of tackling not only *oceanus* but mythical Britain, the Romans again showed true grit in their desire for imperial success at this most north-westerly tip of the known world. Such grit was again on display at the river crossing battle on the Medway when, rebuffed on day one, Plautius used his clever stratagem to seize the initiative on day two. That in itself also presents a lesson, with the legionaries unable to win such a crucial battle on their own and relying on the support of the *auxilia*. This was also the case at the contested crossing of the Thames, where the fleet also played a major role. Such examples show that the Roman military was at its best when all the various arms of the military were combined. Finally, logistics was vital to the success of the Roman legionary blitzkrieg in Britain. In that regard we see Plautius pausing after crossing the Thames to resupply by sea, ensuring there would be no pause once he launched his legionaries northwards once again.

## *The Severan campaigns in Scotland*

In AD 207 the great warrior emperor Septimius Severus was bored in Rome. Having hacked his way to power in the 'Year of Five Emperors' in AD 193, fought two campaigns in the east including the sack of the Parthian capital Ctesiphon, seen off the usurpation of the British governor Clodius Albinus, and campaigned in his native North Africa, he was now reduced to fretting about the behaviour of his sons Caracalla and Geta in the imperial capital. Then a golden opportunity presented itself for one final stab at glory.

Britannia was a troubled province. It had suffered periodic unrest along its northern borders throughout the 2nd century AD, with two major tribal confederations emerging there by its end. These were the Maeatae, based in the central Midland

*The night watchmen. For the majority of the time the legionaries of the Principate led an unglamorous life, policing the borders of the empire. Here on Hadrian's Wall. (Andy Singleton)*

Valley either side of the Clyde–Firth of Forth line, and the Caledonians to their north. In the late AD 190s, with the defences along Hadrian's Wall depleted after Albinus' usurpation attempt, the governor Virius Lupus had been forced to pay huge indemnities to both to prevent further trouble. Such enormous injections of wealth to the northern elites of unconquered Briton, though buying peace in the short term, only further assisted the coalescence of power among their leaders. Trouble again erupted at the beginning of the 3rd century AD though was quickly stamped out, with Lupus and his successors Gaius Valerius Pudens and Lucius Alfenus Senecio then beginning the slow process of rebuilding the northern defences. However, in AD 206/207 a disaster of some kind occurred, with Senecio writing an urgent appeal to Severus saying the province was in danger of being overrun. In it he requested either more troops or the emperor himself. He got both.

Severus' response can be best described as 'shock and awe' writ large. For his *expeditio felicissima Brittannica* he gathered his wife Julia Domna, the squabbling Caracalla and Geta, key senators, courtiers and advisors, the imperial *fiscus* treasury, the Praetorian Guard, legio II Parthica and *vexillations* from

*Heavy metal from legio II Augusta: Principate legionaries with* lorica segmentata *and rectangular* scutum *at the charge. (Andy Singleton)*

all of the crack legions and auxiliary units along the Rhine and Danubian frontiers. The whole were transported to Britain by the Classis Britannica regional fleet in the spring of AD 208, he then establishing York as his imperial capital. There his troops joined the incumbent legio VI Victrix, with the legio II Augusta from Caerleon and legio XX Valeria Victrix from Chester being summoned to join them. In total this gave him an army of 50,000, together with the 7,000 sailors and marines of the regional fleet.

To support this colossal force the fort, harbour and supply base at South Shields was chosen as the main supply depot. This was extended with new immense granaries being built (20 to add to the original two) that could hold 2,500 tonnes of grain, enough to feed the whole force for two months. From here the vessels of the Classis Britannica fulfilled their transport role using the Tyne and well-trodden eastern coastal routes to keep the army supplied once the campaign began, making use of the regional river systems wherever possible. The fort at Corbridge on Dere

*Site of the Roman Antonine fort at Newstead in the Scottish Borders. On the hillside to the rear, Septimius Severus built a 67-hectare marching camp to support his attempts to conquer Scotland in AD 209 and AD 210.*

Street just short of Hadrian's Wall was similarly upgraded, with the granaries there rebuilt even before Severus had arrived (showing the degree of logistical fore planning). Then, in the spring of AD 209, Severus began the first of his two assaults against the Maeatae and Caledonians to the north. He was joined by Caracalla, leaving Geta behind in York to take charge of the Imperial administration.

The huge force marched north from York along Dere Street, crossing Hadrian's Wall and then reaching the Scottish Borders where it destroyed all before it. The whole region was cauterised of opposition. Notably, at this time the Antonine fort at Vindolanda just south of the wall was demolished, with LIA round houses being laid out on a Roman grid pattern there instead. This has been interpreted as a concentration camp for the displaced local population.

The line of march north along Dere Street through the Scottish Borders can be traced by the sequence of enormous 67-hectare marching camps built along its route. These are found at Newstead, St Leonard's (the largest at 70 hectares), Channelkirk and Pathhead. Once again, just as with Plautius' campaign of conquest with his smaller force in the 1st century

AD, the baggage train would have been at the centre of the huge column, with the legionaries and auxiliaries deployed along the flanks and at the front and rear, and with *ala* of cavalry ranging far and wide through the countryside.

Any resistance here would have been in the form of defended settlements such as hill forts, and in that regard one analogy shows the desperate situation the natives found themselves in. This is in the context of recently published research regarding the 7-hectare hill fort site at Burnswark in Dumfresshire. Here, a debate has taken place as to whether data previously considered from antiquarian and 1960s archaeological excavations showed an actual Roman siege from the Antonine period, or a Roman siege training exercise. The key items of interest were the north and south Roman marching camps, and a plethora of ballista bolts/balls and lead slingshots found at the site. To determine the truth the Trimontium Trust recently carried out a review of existing research and fresh data, the latter based on a systematic metal-detecting survey to identify more lead sling shots with a view to plotting their scatter. Experimental archaeology regarding the use of slings in siege warfare was also carried out. The results suggest an actual siege, the two camps seen as a real-world tactical response to the topography and the widespread scatter of sling shots and other missiles (and their quality) suggesting deadly intent. The latter indicates a massive missile barrage, both at the gateways and also along a full half-kilometre of hillfort rampart. The simplest explanation is that the defenders on the hilltop were suppressed by a hail of sling bullets, fired by *auxilia* specialists, with an accurate range of 120 metres and the stopping power of a modern handgun, as well as ballista bolts and arrows. This covered an attacking force of legionaries in *testudo* formation sweeping out the three huge gateways and storming the hilltop. Such a combination of missile troops and legionaries was brutally effective. Further, one other factor adds even more insight into the awful experience of the native Britons on the receiving end of this devastation. This is because some of slingshots were hollowed out with a 4 mm hole through their

*Field surgery in battle, the gruesome side to the life of the legionary.* (Andy Singleton)

centre, designed to make a screeching noise when slung. This is an early example of psychological warfare on the battlefield, bringing to mind the screaming sirens of diving Junkers Ju-87 Stukas during the Blitzkrieg early in World War 2, adding to the misery of those on the receiving end.

The Scottish Borders subdued, Severus reached the Firth of Forth at Inveresk where Dere Street turned west at the River Esk crossing. He then re-established the Antonine fort, supply base and harbour at Cramond and then repaired and re-manned the Antonine Wall to protect his rear. Next he built a bridge of 500 boats at South Queensferry, before dividing the huge force into two legionary spearheads. The larger comprised two thirds of the troops available (likely with the three British legions, used to campaigning in this theatre) under the fitter Caracalla, and a smaller one featuring the Praetorian Guard, other guard units and the legio II Parthica, this under the ailing Severus who was suffering from severe gout. The other units in the overall force, for example the *auxilia*, would have been divided between the two as required.

Caracalla now led his larger force in a *blitzkrieg* lightning strike south-west to north-east along the Highland Boundary Fault, building a sequence of 54-hectare marching camps as he went along to seal off the Highlands from the Maeatae and Caledonians living in the central and northern Midland Valley. The camps were at Househill Dunipace near Falkirk (presumably the stopping-off point before crossing the Forth), Ardoch at the south-western end of the Gask Ridge (where Antonine watch towers may again have been re-manned), Innerpeffray East, Grassy Walls, Cardean, Battledykes, Balmakewan and Kair House. The latter was only 13 kilometres south-west of Stonehaven on the coast, with the Highland line visibly converging with the sea. The plan with these camps was to prevent any Caledonian reserves from emerging into the campaigning theatre from the Highlands. As such, each would have deliberately cut off the glens leading into the Highlands.

With the Highlands and the route northwards to the Moray and Buchan Lowlands beneath the Moray Firth now sealed off, Severus next sent the Classis Britannica along the coast to seal that off also. This left the Maetae and Caledonians in the central and northern Midland Valley in a perilous position, with nowhere to flee. Severus took full advantage, leading a second legionary spearhead with the remaining one third of his force across the bridge of boats on the Firth of Forth again, but this time heading directly north across Fife to the River Tay. This was a region heavily settled by the Maeatae in particular, and to secure it he built two further marching camps, 25 hectares in size, at Auchtermuchty and Edenwood. Reaching the Tay at Carpow he rebuilt and re-manned the Flavian and Antonine fort, supply base and harbour there. This completed his east coast supply route to keep the huge army in the field, featuring South Shields, Cramond and Carpow. He then built another bridge of boats, this time across the Tay, and hammered north into the northern Midland Valley below the Highland line, his legionaries smashing all before them. The conflict there was particularly brutal as the natives refused to gather to allow a definitive set-piece battle to take place (either for tactical reasons, or because they had no chance to coalesce). The campaign therefore became a grinding guerrilla war in the most horrific conditions, with the weather even worse than usual. Both of the key primary sources, Cassius Dio and Herodian, graphically describe the campaign: The former, in his *Roman History*, says (76.13):

> ... as he (Severus) advanced through the country he experienced countless hardships in cutting down the forests, levelling the heights, filling up the swamps, and bridging the rivers; but he fought no battle and beheld no enemy in battle array. The enemy purposely put sheep and cattle in front of the soldiers for them to seize, in order that they might be lured on still further until they were worn out; for in fact the water caused great suffering to the Romans, and when they became scattered, they would be attacked. Then, unable to walk, they would be slain by their own men, in order to avoid capture, so that a full fifty thousand died (clearly a massive exaggeration, but indicative of the difficulties the Romans faced). But Severus did not desist until he approached the extremity of the island.

Meanwhile the latter, in his *History of the Roman Empire*, says (3.14):

> ... frequent battles and skirmishes occurred, and in these the Romans were victorious. But it was easy for the Britons to slip away; putting their knowledge of the surrounding area to good use, they disappeared in the woods and marshes. The Romans' unfamiliarity with the terrain prolonged the war.

Eventually the weight of numbers told and, with the entire regional economy destroyed, the Maetae and Caledonians sued for peace. The resulting treaty was very one-sided in favour of Rome. Severus then proclaimed a famous victory, with he and his two sons being given the title *Britannicus* and celebratory coins being struck to commemorate the event. Campaigning, at least in the short term, was over, and to apparent imperial satisfaction.

*The classic Severan legionary, with* lorica segmentata *and* scutum, *but with the long spear replacing the* pilum.

As always in the Roman experience north of the provincial border though, such a state of comparative calm was not to last.

Severus, Caracalla and the military leadership wintered in York and were still there in early summer AD 210 as a letter dated 5 May in their names was sent from there. However, clearly the terms that had so satisfied the Romans in AD 209 were not so agreeable to at least the Maeatae (probably the recipients of the most extreme experiences of the AD 209 campaign) as in AD 210 they revolted again.

The Caledonians predictably joined in, and Severus determined to go north once more. On this occasion though he had clearly had enough of the troublesome Britons in the far north and gave his famous order to kill all the natives the legionaries came across. The entire campaign was then re-enacted exactly as in AD 210, though wholly under Caracalla as Severus was too ill when the advance began. It was even more brutal than the first, given there was no further unrest on the border for four generations. Archaeological data also shows a de-population event – this indicates something akin to a genocide was committed in the central and upper Midland Valley.

At the end of the campaigning season, whatever was left of the native leadership again sued for peace and were forced to accept even more onerous terms than previously, and the 'severan surge' headed south again to winter near York, leaving significant garrisons in place. However, any plans to remain north of the Solway Firth–Tyne line were cut short when Severus died in York in February AD 211 in the freezing cold of a British winter. Caracalla and Geta, far more interested in establishing their own individual power bases in Rome, quickly left and Severus' 50,000 men gradually returned to their own bases. The northern border was then re-established on Hadrian's wall once more.

A final point to note here is that the British legions seem to have performed particularly well during the Severan campaigns in Scotland, with for example legio VI being awarded the commemorative title 'Britannica Pia Fidelis' (based on tile stamps from Carpow) and legio XX being similarly styled *Antoniniana* by Caracalla after the death of his father.

# In battle

Having looked at the legionary on campaign to see how the Roman military operated at a strategic level, I now focus on their experiences in battle to examine their tactical use in close detail. To provide such an overview I have chosen three specific engagements that book-end the empire chronologically, these being Caesar's victory over Pompey at Pharsalus in 48 BC, Gaius Suetonius Paulinus' defeat of Boudicca in AD 61 and the emperor Julian's victory over the Alamanni in AD 357. The first, from immediately prior to the Principate Empire, shows how the legionaries performed when evenly matched with their opponents given this was legionary versus legionary. The second shows the legionary fighting against great odds and still winning through, detailing why this was so often the case. The third is illustrative of how the legionaries performed in a late Roman Dominate context. Finally I examine the Severan campaign in Scotland again to show how the legionary defeated opponents who specifically avoided a meeting engagement through the use of guerrilla tactics, a common occurrence in the Principate and Dominate.

## *The battle of Pharsalus*

Pharsalus, in Thessaly in north-eastern Greece, was the location of the decisive battle in 48 BC between Caesar and Pompey at the height of the civil wars of the 1st century BC. Previous encounters between the two had been indecisive and matters would now come to a head in the largest encounter between Romans armies to that date.

The campaigning theatre was chosen by Pompey who fled Italy in 49 BC rather than confront Caesar. He believed some of the local legions there would side with his younger rival. This reflected the autonomous nature of the Marian legions, each of which had a very distinct sense of identity and loyalty.

Caesar almost caught Pompey as he left Brindisi (Roman *Brundisium*) in southern Italy but he escaped, heading for Greece where he began to gather his legions. Caesar then targeted Pompey's seven legions in Spain to neutralise the threat to his rear before he looked to Greece. There Pompey had made Beroea his headquarters where he mustered nine legions and many allied troops armed in their native fashion, for example cavalry, archers and slingers. He also gathered a large fleet of 600 ships.

Back in Italy Caesar struggled to get the backing of the ruling classes who had made Pompey the commander-in-chief of the republic's armies. The latter decided to defend the western coast of Greece from any attempt by Caesar to land his army there and moved westwards from Thessaly, establishing a winter camp on arrival. Then, late in the campaigning season, Caesar surprised all. Defying Pompey's naval supremacy, he determined to risk a winter crossing from Italy and mustered as many legionaries as he could, sailing on 4 January. He left his baggage train behind to save time and landed without incident at Palaeste, having avoided Pompey's fleet stationed on Corcyra (modern Corfu). He then drew Pompey out of his winter quarters by sacking the nearby cities nominally under the latter's protection, the two forces facing off either side of the River Apsus in Illyria. There they would remain for four months.

Caesar's second-in-command Mark Antony arrived in April with reinforcements, boosting the number of Caesar's legions to 11. The two forces now broke camp, Pompey heading back to Thessaly and Caesar following. There they faced off again at Asparagium. Despite outnumbering his opponent Pompey still refused to force an engagement, confident he could harass Caesar's lines of supply. He then moved again, this time to the coast at Dyrrachium. Caesar now began an audacious project to build an enclosing wall around Pompey's camp to box it against the sea. Realising the danger Pompey countered quickly by sallying out with his troops, forcing Caesar to retreat. Pompey then established a new camp south of Caesar's siege fortifications, threatening the latter's rear. However on 9 July, when Pompey's forces were split between Dyrrachium and the new camp, Caesar attacked the former. Pompey was forced to send five of his legions to extricate the trapped troops. Both sides suffered many losses, particularly Caesar, but the action proved indecisive.

Caesar now abandoned the blockade and withdrew south, concerned at the increasing disparity in numbers as Pompey continued to receive reinforcements from his allies in the east. Pompey's cavalry pursued but Caesar escaped to Thessaly, setting up camp on the north bank of the River Enipeus between Pharsalus and Palaepharsalus. Pompey followed with his whole force and set up his own camp a kilometre to the west. For this he chose a range of low hills, these providing a good strategic position ensuring a safe route for supplies to reach him from the coast. The two armies again faced off.

Both armies featured a core of legions together with allies, though Pompey had the greater force and slightly more allies. By this time Caesar had with him elements of nine of his legions numbering some 23,000 legionaries in 80 cohorts (many of which were under-strength). He also had between 5,000 and 10,000 allied foot and around 1,000 Gallic and German cavalry. Pompey had elements of 12 legions together with seven cohorts of legionaries from Spain, in total numbering 50,000. He also had 4,200 allied foot and 7,000 allied horse.

Caesar, clearly outnumbered, was keen to settle the issue immediately. However Pompey, on the range of hills, was unwilling to abandon his advantage of high ground, despite the weight of numbers in his favour. Several days passed before Caesar decided to fall back in the hope of drawing Pompey from his camp. On the morning of 9 August Pompey took the bait and moved his troops out onto the plain. Caesar pounced immediately, abandoning his baggage and even destroying his own field defences to get more of his legionaries onto the battlefield.

Pompey was the first to begin deploying, with 110 cohorts of legionaries plus line-of-battle allies lined up along a 4-kilometre front in the *triplica acies* formation. This was a repeating succession of four cohorts in the first line and three in each of the second and third lines. He deployed most of his cavalry, archers and slingers on his left flank up hard against the low hills where his camp was, with a smaller cavalry and light infantry force on the right against the River Enipeus. His veteran legionaries were dispersed throughout his force to support newly recruited troops. Pompey's plan was for his cavalry to circle around Caesar's flanks and attack his rear while his infantry pinned Caesar's centre. Pompey positioned himself at the rear of the left wing.

Meanwhile Caesar, beginning his deployment later, lined up his troops parallel to Pompey's but with his three lines somewhat thinner given his numerical disadvantage. He was keen to avoid a hanging flank that Pompey's legionaries could exploit. Next he positioned himself opposite Pompey, behind the veteran and highly motivated legio X, the best legion on the field. He then deployed his cavalry on his right, and to harass the opposing legionaries positioned his light missile troops across his centre. As a precaution against Pompey's superior cavalry numbers he also moved six cohorts of legionaries from his rear line, positioning them as a reserve on his extreme right flank at an oblique angle.

The armies now closed to within 140 metres and faced off, Pompey then ordering the first attack with his cavalry where he held the numerical advantage. Caesar's cavalry counter-charged and a melee ensued. Meanwhile, Caesar's first two lines of infantry approached Pompey's foot who stood their ground rather than advancing to meet the oncoming enemy. Seeing Pompey's lines were not advancing, Caesar halted his legions just out of range of the legionaries' lighter *pila*. He then redressed his ranks, before ordering a charge by his first two lines (the third being held in reserve). The legionaries surged forward, each unleashing both *pila* before drawing their *gladius* and closing. Pompey's legionaries countered, both sides finally meeting in a savage crescendo.

On the left flank Pompey's cavalry were beginning to make their weight of numbers tell and Caesar ordered his mounted troops to withdraw, leaving Pompey in control of the flank. However Caesar now ordered his right flank reserve of six cohorts forward to engage Pompey's cavalry who were re-forming. They charged to close quarters, hurling their *pila* into the faces of their opponents who broke in short order. The republican cavalry fled the field in confusion, leaving Caesar in control of the whole flank.

In the centre Caesar now committed his third line to prevent Pompey from redeploying his own legionaries. He then wheeled the six cohorts on his right into the exposed left flank of Pompey's legionaries. Butchery ensued and Pompey's army broke, the allied troops fleeing first before the legionaries routed. The latter retreated headlong for the hills, with Pompey retreating to his camp before leaving the field completely. The one-time champion of the republic now rode for Larissa with a small escort, disguising himself as an ordinary soldier.

Caesar was relentless in his pursuit. He wiped out Pompey's camp, causing what was left of Pompey's legions to flee to a hill called the Kaloyiros. This he besieged, and eventually Pompey's remaining legions, leaderless, surrendered. Caesar claimed to have killed 15,000 of his opponents, losing 1,200 himself. Pompey never recovered, fleeing to Egypt where he was beheaded on arrival.

What is clear from the primary sources regarding this battle is that the élan of Caesar's legions, particularly legio X, more than made up for their numerical disadvantage. Pompey, dubbed 'the Great' by contemporaries, was far from it in this campaign and once Caesar's had destroyed his rival's left flank, the command and control he excised over his legions ensured the republican army was quickly rolled up. Caesar also made much better use of reserves, knowing that with the legionaries of both sides evenly matched (at least in terms of equipment) the ability to exploit success would be vital. So it proved.

## The defeat of Boudicca

The most famous event in the story of the Roman occupation of Britain is the blood-soaked rebellion of Boudicca in AD 60/61. This almost ended the Roman presence in the islands and saw the legionaries fighting in the most extreme of conditions. Defeat would have meant destruction of four whole legions, on a scale even larger than the loss of the three legions in the Teutoburg Forest in AD 9. That the legionaries won through is testament to their morale, training and fitness.

By the late AD 50s, through a series of lightning campaigns, the legionary spearheads had defeated all opposition in the south, east and the midlands of Britain. In the north the Brigantes, allies of Rome, kept the peace. This just left Wales, where the governor Gauis Suetonius Paulinus was mounting a gruelling campaign in difficult conditions and terrain. His target was the north-west of the peninsula, specifically Anglesey deep in the heart of Deceangli territory. This mysterious island was home to the druids, leaders of LIA religion in pre-Roman Britain and the emotive centre of any remaining resistance to Rome. In AD

60 he made an amphibious assault there. This was a Claudian invasion in miniature using specially built flat-bottomed transport boats to cope with the treacherous coastal currents and shallows around the island. Though the fighting was desperate, Paulinus was ultimately successful and Anglesey captured.

However, the governor's attempt to consolidate was cut short by the revolt of Boudicca, queen of the Iceni in northern East Anglia. The context behind this dramatic event was the earlier death of the Iceni king Prasutagus, Boudicca's husband. He was an ally of Rome who in his will left his kingdom to both his daughters and Emperor Nero. However, when he died this was ignored and the kingdom annexed by Rome. The primary sources say Boudicca protested but was flogged and her daughters raped for her trouble, though one adds that another factor was Roman financiers calling in their loans to the British elites.

Whatever the cause, the queen rebelled. Soon the Iceni were joined by all their regional neighbours, keen to break free of the shackles of Rome. An enormous column 100,000 strong (mostly families and camp followers rather than warriors) now marched south. First they destroyed the provincial capital Colchester, a *colonia* built on the site of the previous Catuvellauni capital Camulodunum. This was a particularly brutal event, many of the Romans unaware of the danger until it was too late. A large number were burned alive as they sought shelter in the Temple of Claudius, built to celebrate Plautius' earlier victory.

The Roman military did try to intervene at this point, with the future governor Quintus Petilius Cerialis leading *vexillations* of the legio IX Hispana (of which he was a legate) to intercept Boudicca. His small force arrived too late to save Colchester and was then decisively defeated by the main British army, he fleeing for his life with his cavalry. They remained incongruously holed up in a nearby fort until after the insurrection had been defeated.

Boudicca then razed the new *municipia* (merchant town) of St Albans. Finally she headed for London, recently founded as a major trading port on the River Thames. This had no defences at all, though there was enough time for those who could to flee to the continent. For those who couldn't the result was predictable and another massacre occurred. The primary sources say that 80,000 Romans and Romano-British were killed from the point Boudicca had headed south, most in the three sacked towns. However the stage was now set for Roman retribution on a devastating scale.

In Wales, Paulinus abandoned his assault on the druids as soon as he heard of the revolt. He immediately headed south-east along the route of Watling Street. He was accompanied by his own legion, the legio XIV Gemina, together with *vexillations* of legio XX Valeria Victrix and a few auxiliary units including two *ala* of cavalry. He also sent for the Exeter-based legio II Augusta but the unit's commander and tribunes were away and its *praefectus castrorum* (camp prefect, the third in command) Poenius Postumus ignored the call, bringing shame on the legion. Meanwhile, some stragglers of the legio IX Hispana may have found their way to Paulinus. In total the governor was able to field an army of 6,000 legionaries, 4,000 foot auxiliaries and around 1,000 mounted auxiliaries.

Boudicca now moved to intercept Paulinus along Watling Street, wanting to bring matters to a swift conclusion. Of her 100,000 (some sources saying this had grown to 230,000) she could muster perhaps 60,000 warriors, giving her an immense superiority in numbers. She knew that if the governor was defeated, the Romans might abandon the province for good and so pressed hard for a meeting engagement. She knew what to expect if the Romans won, thus the forthcoming battle would be an all or nothing clash for both sides.

Paulinus chose the place to make his stand very carefully, in a steep defile with woods on either side and rear. These protected his flanks and limited the frontage of the line of battle, negating the British superiority in numbers and playing to the martial superiority of his own legionaries. The location of the battle is unknown, with most historians and archaeologists favouring a site either in the West Midlands or near St Albans along Watling Street, though a recent theory has suggested High Cross in Leicestershire. Here Watling Street met the Fosse Way (linking

Lincoln to Exeter) and would have allowed the legio II Augusta to quickly join Paulinus if the legion had obeyed orders.

Paulinus deployed his legionaries and *auxilia* uphill of the Britons in four main bodies at his centre and left and right flanks, and with a reserve to the rear of the centre. He then positioned an *ala* of auxiliary cavalry on either flank hard against the woods there. Boudicca deployed her enormous force opposite, though in much denser formation, with chariots in front manned by her own elite warriors. The Britons were so confident of victory that the families of the warriors now joined the baggage train at the rear of her line to watch events unfold.

Boudicca exhorted her army to more slaughter and then opened the battle with a wild charge of both the chariots and her warriors. The former rode across the front of the Romans, hurling javelins and insults, before turning square on to close for hand-to-hand combat. The foot troops followed close behind. The discipline of the legionaries now shone through. En masse they released their lighter *pila*, 6,000 iron-barbed javelins arcing high in the air in a steep parabola before dropping on the heads of the Britons. The auxiliary infantry joined in with their own javelins, and with slings wielded by specialist missile troops. Then, at point-blank range, the legionaries unleashed their second, heavier *pila*. These were thrown in a flat arc, hammering into the front ranks of Britons who came to a shuddering halt in a tangle of dead horses, overturned chariots, bodies and wounded.

Paulinus saw his chance and seized the initiative. The legionaries now moved forward in a series of *cuneus* (swine head) wedge formations, centurions and standard bearers to the fore. *Gladius* were drawn and *scutum* set hard forward. The wedges charged downhill into the sprawling mass of Britons, causing slaughter everywhere and forcing the Britons into so dense a mass that the warriors were unable to use their weapons. A massacre ensued as the Britons broke and tried to run away. However they were trapped on the field by the surrounding families and baggage train. All were hacked down where they stood, the legionaries giving no quarter.

The result was an immense victory for Paulinus, he losing only 400 men to the Britons 80,000. Boudicca poisoned herself, leaving the revolt leaderless. The Romans then drafted in 2,000 more legionaries from Germany, together with 1,000 auxiliary cavalry and eight units of auxiliary foot, to help stamp out the last flames of resistance. This was carried out with such vigour in the Iceni homelands of north Norfolk that the region remained for many years under-developed compared to the rest of the south and the east of the province.

Thus ended the Boudiccan revolt, with the province secure for another 340 years. The battle that crushed the rebellion is particularly illustrative of the martial capabilities of the Principate legionary, particularly the discipline required first to withstand the terrifying charge of the Britons, and then to maintain the wedge formations as they stamped and stabbed their way forward to victory. One other result also shows the fate of those who let their troops down, for back in Exeter the cowardly Postumus took his own life.

## The battle of Strasbourg

Also known as the battle of Argentoratum, this engagement fought in AD 357 shows the evolution of the legionary into a warrior very different from that of the Principate at its height (as detailed in Chapters 2 and 5). Now clad in a thigh-length mail shirt and with flat oval body shield and sturdy iron helmet, he was a spearman fighting in a deep formation not that dissimilar to the Tullian phalanx. He was also part of a combined-arms force, less reliant on heavy foot and with a much larger mounted component. Yet he still had a key role to play, as will be seen.

This battle was the culmination of the war between the western Roman army under the *Caesar* (junior emperor) Julian and the Alamanni tribal confederation led by their senior king, Chnodomar. The conflict had begun in AD 355 when Julian moved to evict the marauding Germans from Gaul and restore

## Known governors of Roman Britain

| AD 43 | Aulus Plautius |
|---|---|
| AD 47 | Publius Ostorius Scapula |
| AD 52 | Didius Gallus |
| AD 57 | Quintus Veranius |
| AD 58 | Gaius Suetonius Paulinus |
| AD 61 | Publius Petronius Turpilianus |
| AD 63 | Marcus Trebellius Maximus |
| AD 69 | Marcus Vettius Bolanus |
| AD 71 | Quintus Petilius Cerialis |
| AD 74 | Sextus Julius Frontinus |
| AD 77 | Gnaeus Julius Agricola |
| AD 98 | Publius Metilius Nepos Titus Avidius Quietus |
| AD 103 | Lucius Neratius Marcellus |
| AD 115 | Marcus Atilius Bradua |
| AD 122 | Aulus Platorius Nepos |
| AD 126 | Lucius Trebius Germanus |
| AD 131 | Sextus Julius Severus |
| AD 133 | Publius Mummius Sisenna |
| AD 138 | Quintus Lollius Urbicus |
| AD 145 | Gnaeus Papirus Aelianus |
| AD 157 | Gnaeus Julius Verus |
| AD 162 | Marcus Statius Priscus Sextus Calpurnius Agricola |
| AD 174 | Caerellius |
| AD 178 | Ulpius Marcellus |
| AD 185 | Publius Helvius Pertinax. |
| AD 191 / 192 | Decimus Clodius Albinus |
| AD 197 | Virius Lupus |
| AD 202 | Gaius Valerius Pudens |
| AD 205 | Lucius Alfenus Senecio |
| AD 216 | Marcus Antonius Gordianus (Britannia Inferior) |

| AD 222 | Tiberius Julius Pollienus Auspex (Britannia Superior) |
| AD 223 | Claudius Xenophon (Britannia Inferior) |
| AD 225 | Maximus (Britannia Inferior) |
| AD 226 | Calvisius Rufus (Britannia Inferior) |
| | Valerius Crescens (Britannia Inferior) |
| | Claudius Appelinus (Britannia Inferior) |
| AD 237 | Tuccianus (Britannia Inferior) |
| AD 238 | Marcus Martiannius Pulcher (Britannia Superior) |
| | Maecilius Fuscus (Britannia Inferior) |
| | Egnatius Lucilianus (Britannia Inferior) |
| AD 242 | Nonius Philippus (Britannia Inferior) |
| AD 244 | Aemilianus (Britannia Inferior) |
| AD 253 | Desticius Juba (Britannia Superior) |
| AD 262 | Octavius Sabinus (Britannia Inferior) |

Vicarius

| AD 319 | Pacatianus |
| AD 351 | Flavius Martinus |
| AD 358 | Alypius |
| AD 367 | Civilis |
| AD 395 | Chrysanthus |
| AD 400 | Victorinus |

the *limes Germanicus* along the Rhine. This had been largely destroyed during the civil wars of AD 350–353.

The Alamanni were originally from the Main valley in central Germany. They came into contact with Rome when they colonised the *Agri Decumates* region in modern Baden-Wurttemburg in south-west Germany after this was evacuated by the Romans in the mid-3rd century AD (it had been part of province of Germania Superior for 150 years). In the AD 350s they established a series of cantons on the eastern bank of the Rhine from where they began launching substantial raids across the river into the empire, taking advantage of the political turmoil there. The level of raiding increased as the decade progressed, and they eventually began to settle on the western side of the river, drawing the attention of the *Caesar.*

Julian's task was daunting. The preceding civil war had left Gaul in chaos, with many key towns in German hands including Mainz, Worms, Speyer, Saverne, Brumat and Strasbourg. Only Cologne (Roman Colonia Agrippina) with its massive fortifications, and three other strongpoints on the Rhine, were still under Roman control. Meanwhile in the interior, large bands and Alamanni and other German tribes such as the Franks were roaming the countryside, pillaging at will. Some reached as far as the River Seine.

By this time, the Roman military were divided into two principal troop types, the *comitatenses* field army troops and the *limitanei* border troops. Although the latter could be fielded in the line of battle (those so doing branded *pseudocomitatenses* warriors), more often than not they were effectively gendarmes manning the borders. There they acted as a trip wire, tasked with delaying any incursions until the nearest *comitatenses* field army arrived.

Julian was ordered to secure the Rhine border by the *Augustus* (full emperor) Constantius II, his kinsman. He travelled from Milan where he was given a guard of 200 *scholae palitinae* Imperial household cavalry, a regiment of 600 *cataphractarii* fully armoured (man and horse) lancers, and some bow armed *equites Sagittarius* light cavalry. This formed the core of his field army. En route north he then received word that Cologne had fallen, and that all of the regional *limitanei* had been overpowered and destroyed by the Germans.

Julian spent the winter of AD 355/356 in Vienna (Roman Vienne), in the spring heading north for Reims (Roman Remi) where the regional *magister militum* Marcellus (senior commander) had gathered the remaining *comitatenses* units from across Gaul. Julian's journey was fraught with danger as it involved a long march through countryside swarming with German raiding parties, all larger than his own mounted escort. He reached Reims though, on the way rescuing Autun (Roman *Augustodunum*) from a German force trying to invest the town. This was a particularly important location as it was home to a number of the state-run *fabricae* manufactories that made much of the military equipment for the region.

At Reims Julian decided to tackle the Alamanni issue at source by marching north once more, heading directly for the border. He first targeted Alsace, losing one minor engagement on the way and winning another. Reaching the Rhine he realised his force was too small to take on the main Alamanni force alone. Instead he headed for Cologne to recover it for Rome, finding it in ruins when he arrived. He set his legionaries and *auxilia* the task of rebuilding the town walls, and then signed a peace treaty with the Franks who had been raiding with the Alemanni. This allowed him to concentrate on the latter.

He spent the winter of AD 356–357 in Sens (Roman Senones) near Paris, quartering his troops across the regional towns to spread the burden of their maintenance given the precarious nature of the local economy. The Alamanni heard of this and besieged him in Sens, he only having his cavalry with him, but they withdrew after a month. He then sacked Marcellus who had failed to come to his aid, replacing him with another, more amenable senior officer called Severus.

Constantius, always wary of his cousin, now intervened. A plan was drawn up to trap the Alamanni in eastern Gaul using a pincer movement. In this, Julian would advance eastward from Reims, while a major field army of 25,000 from Italy under the *magister* Barbatio would head to Augst (Roman Augusta Rauracorum) in Raetia. The idea was to catch the main Alamanni force in Alsace between the two Roman armies.

However large bands of Alamanni ignored the threat and invaded the rich Rhone valley, even trying to take the major regional town of Lyon (Roman Lugdunum). This bold move left them trapped in the interior of Gaul, with two Roman armies advancing to their rear. Julian, realising the Germans would try to escape north, despatched squadrons of cavalry to lie in ambush on the three main regional roads. These successfully intercepted and destroyed many of the returning bands of Alamanni. However in Barbatio's sector the main body of Germans were allowed to pass through unmolested, reaching the Rhine near Strasbourg where they set up camps on islands in the river. Julian was furious. He immediately headed north and assaulted one of the islands, wiping out the German camp there. The remaining Alamanni now retreated onto the eastern bank, abandoning their remaining island camps and much of the loot they had dragged across the length of Gaul.

Julian now set about rebuilding the fortress at Saverne (Roman Tres Tabernae), which had been destroyed by the Germans. This key base sat astride the vital Metz (Roman Mediomatrici) to Strasbourg trunk road, the site also commanding the heights overlooking the Rhine valley there. Barbatio meanwhile led his force into an ambush by a strong Alamanni force that had re-crossed the river. His vanguard fled in disarray and the *magister* panicked. He ordered his army into a hasty retreat, closely pursued by the Germans. He then completely lost his nerve and headed south across the Alps, aiming to winter in northern Italy despite it being the middle of the campaigning season, leaving Julian to face the entire Alamanni force alone and sabotaging the pincer strategy.

Chnodomar, now free to roam northern Gaul again, targeted Julian's refortification of Saverne. He ordered a mass mobilisation of all the confederation's member tribes that gathered at Strasbourg. With other Germans soon joining, this gave him a large army of around 35,000, including all the other Alamanni kings. He then provoked Julian into action by sending him an ultimatum to evacuate Alsace immediately or be wiped out.

The *Caesar's* safer option was to ignore Chnodomar's challenge and keep his troops in their fortified bases until Constantius sent reinforcements. However he now doubted these would come given Barbatio's earlier performance. In effect he had now become the trapped force. He therefore resolved to fight Chnodomar alone, with the backing of Florentius, the *praefectus praetorio Galliarum* (governor-general of Gaul) who was keen to get his provinces there back under his control.

Julian set out at dawn on a hot August day, leading his army of around 13,000 to within sight of Chnodomar's fortified camp near Strasbourg. He then gave a speech to the men, suggesting they camp overnight and engage the Alemanni the following day when fresh. The troops would have none of it though, demanding immediate action. The *Caesar* consented and they advanced on the Germans.

Chnodomar now deployed his large army from its camp, choosing to face Julian on a gently sloping hill a few miles from the Rhine where the fields were ripe with wheat. The western edge of the battlefield was defined by the Metz–Strasbourg Roman highway, on the far side of which was broken and wooded terrain impassable to Julian's cavalry. The Alamanni left wing was directly commanded by Chnodomar and his own guard cavalry, among whom he scattered lightly armed infantry concealed among the standing wheat. The German right wing sat on the highway, while in the rough terrain beyond the road a further substantial force was hidden in ambush. This wing was commanded by Chnodomar's nephew Serapio. The centre, where the majority of the Alamanni stood atop the crest of the hill, was divided up into various tribes under their own kings (five major and ten minor such leaders are listed as present by the primary sources).

Julian positioned his infantry in two lines, widely spaced apart and up to 16 ranks deep (spearmen for the most part, with archers at the rear). The second line would be deployed to exploit any successes, or to counter any enemy breakthroughs on the flanks or to their front.

The front line included troops from four legions, by now differently named from those of the Principate. These were the Moesiaci, Pannoniaci, Iovani and Herculiani, numbering 4,000 in total. Either side in the same line were deployed units of elite auxiliaries, the *auxilia palatina*. By this time in the later Dominate such troops were equipped exactly the same as the legionaries, and in some cases had reputations even more distinguished as warriors. Units present at Strasbourg in this front line were called the Petulantes, Heruli, Cornuti and Brachiati, numbering 2,000 in total. In the rear line was another legion, the Primani, numbering 1,000, together with more *auxilia palatina* troops from the Celtae, Batavi and Regae units, these totalling 2,000 men. On his left flank Julian deployed 2,000 more auxiliaries under Severus across the Metz–Strasbourg road, while on his right he deployed his cavalry including the heavily armoured cataphracts. Julian positioned himself between the two lines of foot.

As soon as the two armies were drawn up the German warriors demanded that Chnodomar and his guards should dismount and lead the Alamanni foot from the centre, which he did. Julian then opened the engagement by sending his horse archers forward to harass the densely packed German warriors to his front. He next ordered his right wing shock cavalry forward, led by the cataphracts, who charged the German horse. As they entered the wheat fields these were ambushed by the German light troops hiding there, and when the German cavalry counter-charged the Roman horse broke. In their headlong flight they almost hit the Roman right-wing infantry in the first line, but these held their ground and the cavalry were rallied behind the foot by Julian himself.

The Germans, seeing the Roman cavalry on their left run, now charged en masse. Led by Chnodomar and the other Alamanni kings, they repeatedly crashed into the Roman front line of foot. The well-trained legionaries and *auxilia palatina* met each wave in the same way, the spearmen throwing clouds of javelins and darts (see Chapter 5) before setting their spears and shields to meet the Alamanni warriors, bowmen at their rear showering arrows over their heads into the German ranks. Finally though the pressure told, a wedge of Alamanni led by a number of kings punching through the first Roman line, thousands of Germans pouring through the gap. However the units either side held firm, and

Julian now led the legionaries of the Primani forward from the second line to contain the breach. The move was successful and the Germans were pushed back. Now exhausted and suffering severe losses, the Alamanni were pushed back, particularly on the wings of the battle line (on the extreme Roman left Severus had already forced the Germans from the field). Pushed into a denser and denser mass, unable to wield their weapons, the Alamanni finally broke and fled the field, many cut down by the pursuing Roman cavalry. A large number tried to swim across the Rhine but many drowned, weighed down by armour or hit by Roman missiles. Around 8,000 perished on the battlefield, and many more in the river. Julian lost just over 200, making this a great victory for the *Caesar*. Chnodomar was later captured, dying in Rome from disease while a prisoner.

This battle shows the field army legionaries and *auxilia palatina* of the late Dominate at the height of their powers. Once again discipline was a key to their success, with the first line of foot standing firm firstly when the Roman right-wing cavalry broke, and then when the same line was pierced by repeated German attacks. Once that occurred, the second line also remained steady, advancing to plug the gap and ensuring ultimate victory. Just as with the legions of the Principate, the élan of these later Roman warriors won the day.

## Guerrilla warfare

The legionaries of Rome had such a fearsome reputation that often their opponents chose not to stand up to them in a set-piece battle but instead engaged them in guerrilla warfare. Such asymmetrical conflict was a key feature of the Severan campaigns of AD 209 and AD 210 in Scotland, offering an intriguing glimpse of how the Roman military countered this style of conflict. Both of these campaigns were grim for all of the protagonists. The weather was worse than usual, even in the far north of the islands of Britain, and the terrain proved particularly difficult for the

Romans. Cassius Dio provides great insight here into the nature of the Maeatae and Caledonians, saying (77.12.1-4):

> Both tribes inhabit wild and waterless mountains and desolate and swampy plains, and possess neither walls, cities, nor tilled fields, but live on their flocks, wild game, and certain fruits... They can endure hunger and cold and any kind of hardship; for they plunge into swamps and exist there for many days with only their heads above water, and in forests they support themselves upon bark and roots, and for all emergencies they prepare a certain kind of food, the eating of a small portion of which, the size of a bean, prevents them from feeling either hunger or thirst.

The hunger-preventing food described here has been identified as the heath pea by Dr Brian Moffat of the Soutra Aisle research centre.

It is clear from the above that the natives of the far north of Britain proved a desperate opponent for the Romans, with their guerrilla tactics telling '... against the Romans and prolonged the war' according to Herodian (3.14). They were clearly far more experienced to a life of living rough in their indigenous terrain when required, with Herodian (3.14) adding that they dispensed with breast plates and helmets 'which would impede their movement through the marshes.'

All these references illustrate the guerrilla warfare used by the native British opposition and it is perhaps useful to look elsewhere chronologically and geographically for analogies to see how the legionaries would have responded. The Roman military was well experienced at fighting such campaigns, particularly in Britain given the asymmetry between their own forces and those of the natives (this was not the case against the Parthians in the east for example). This would also have been the case for Severus in North Africa earlier in his reign where he engaged the Garamantes tribe who were similarly symmetrically disadvantaged against the Romans, and this previous campaign would certainly have made an impression on the emperor, the lessons learned later being deployed in Scotland.

Roman military textbooks detail how to conduct such a specialist style of warfare, for example former British 1st-century AD warrior governor Frontinus (1.6.3) explaining in his *Strategemata* (*Stratagems*) how to deal with ambushes using classical world examples:

> When Iphicrates was leading his army in Thrace in a long file on account of the nature of the terrain, and the report was brought to him that the enemy planned to attack his rear-guard, he ordered some cohorts to withdraw to both flanks and halt, while the rest were to quicken their pace and flee. But from the complete line as it passed by, he kept back all the choicest soldiers. Thus, when the enemy were busy with promiscuous pillaging, and in fact were already exhausted, while his own men were refreshed and drawn up in order, he attacked and routed the foe and stripped them of their booty.

What seems clear from these primary sources is that, despite the difficulties pinning down their opponents (who were clearly fighting for survival in the case of Severus in Scotland), the Romans always adapted to the tactics being used against them, even if often at great cost. Such adaption to the circumstances was one of the great characteristics of the Roman military, they relying on their sophisticated organisation, training, élan and well organised supply system to eventually give them an advantage in all kinds of warfare, including against an opponent who avoided confrontation. In particular, the legionaries would destroy the local economy, employing slash-and-burn tactics to deprive the natives of their homes and food. In the AD 210 campaign in Scotland this reached its peak with Severus' order to kill all the natives the legionaries came across. Thus, while things were grim for the Romans in these campaigns, they overcame the adversity and ensured that the discomfort felt by all levels of native northern British society (whose local economy was destroyed in the first year of campaigning) was far more brutal.

# CHAPTER 4

# NON-CONFLICT ROLES OF THE ROMAN LEGIONARY

The legionary was not just a warrior. He was also an administrator, policeman, fire fighter, helped run agriculture and industry, and an outstanding engineer and builder.

## Administration

The main political force in the Roman Empire was the state. This was intricately involved in every economic activity, usually geared to supporting its continuance and infrastructure. It was a patrician institution with responsibilities including political, economic and social roles that were often related. To carry these out, in an age before a civil service, nationalised industries and a free market economy able to fund major capital expenditure projects, it turned to the only tool at its disposal, namely the military. This was the largest institution within the empire, and it was in this capacity that the Roman military was the central instrument used by the emperor to ensure the smooth running of the imperial system.

Such administration activities would have been a key function for the military in a given province. This was because, even when combining the governor's and procurator's staffs, there were only

80 or fewer senior officials to run the province. A comparison with Britain's modern civil service is useful here, where over 25 per cent of the population are in public sector jobs of one kind or another, more in some areas.

As administrators the military would have been at their most visible in a newly conquered territory where they exercised very wide powers. These included the ability to carry out summary justice and to impose restrictions on the movement of the native population. It is at this early stage of occupation that we also see the legionary overtly operating as administrators for the first time in the new land. This was in their capacity as skilled military land surveyors, able to quickly survey the new territory. This allowed a rapid assessment of its likely contribution to the emperor's *fiscus*.

Once established within the empire, legionaries of all ranks could then be seconded to the governor's *officium consularis,* the main body used to govern a province. These were called *beneficiarii consularis* and helped bolster his staff given the limited number of civilians at his disposal. Governors also often deployed such *beneficiarii* to command the operation of way-stations on the major trunk routes of the empire. Here they acted as the governor's local representative, fulfilling a variety of roles including the enforcement of tax collection, escorting officials and controlling traffic.

The *beneficiarii* were also employed more broadly in administrative roles across the provinces by governors. We have a number of very specific examples in the historical record and epigraphy, for example in Britain. These include the cavalry prefect Titus Haterius Nepos who is detailed carrying out a census in Annandale in Dumfries and Galloway around AD 117. Other examples include centurions such as T. Floridius Natalis of legio VI Victrix performing the role of regional administrator at Ribchester, and C. Severius Emeritus of legio II Augusta who performed a similar role in Bath. In such roles they ensured the efficient operation of the imperial administrative system.

Finally, the legions also included their own administrative specialists in addition to the *beneficiarii* seconded to the governor's staff. Such clerical legionaries were drawn from the ranks and performed roles within the legions that included keeping grain store records and managing the financial accounts of the troops. Called *immunes librarii,* they can be found across the empire, for example Septimius Licinius of legio II Parthica, who set up a commemoration to a daughter in Albano, Italy, and Marcus Uplius Firminus, who similarly set up an inscription in Potaissa (modern Torda), Dacia.

## Policing

Legionaries were also used in a policing capacity across the empire. This is most evident in the east where for much of the Principate the legions were often located near major urban centres such as Alexandria. Here, the two-legion garrison of Egypt was based at the legionary fortress of Nikopolis, close to the provincial capital. Meanwhile, the Classis Alexandrina regional fleet was based in the city itself. Given their size, such cities often experienced turbulent unrest and the military presence there was frequently deployed to restore order with violent force.

Elsewhere in the empire, for example in Britain, we also see the proximity of the military to a civilian population reflected in the context of policing. A prime example is the Cripplegate *vexillation*-size fort in London, built during the reign of Hadrian as a response (it has recently been argued) to some kind of insurrection. Another example presents in northern Italy where Emperor Tiberius sent a cohort of legionaries to deal with an unspecified scandalous incident in the town of Pollentia. The troops surrounded the town and imprisoned most of the adult population who were given life sentences in prison. Meanwhile a praetorian cohort was similarly used by Nero to stamp out insurrection in Puteoli in Campania in AD 58. The military was also of course the force deployed to deal with slave revolts. Tiberius for example dispatched a force to deal with such an incident in southern Italy in AD 24.

It was also the norm for legionaries to carry out other types of policing in addition to using brute force to keep the emperor's peace. Whether reporting to the governor or local magistracy, we have direct evidence for these military personnel being so deployed. For example a document from Egypt dated AD 207 details a centurion named Aurelius Julius Marcellinus being contacted by a woman called Aurelia Tisais who claimed her father and brother had been murdered on a hunting trip. Another document, dated AD 193, has a centurion called Ammonius Paternus being contacted by a man known as Syros with regard to the abuse of tax collection.

In all of these roles the legionaries bolstered the regular urban gendarmerie. In the cities and towns of the empire these were called *cohorts urbanae*, of which Rome had six cohorts, and *vigils urbani* city watchmen.

## Firefighting

Firefighting was another public function of the legionary, again usually in the context of deployment in the urban environment. A prime example are the two cohorts permanently stationed at Ostia to guard against fire at the key port facilities there. This was an essential function for the warriors given the vital grain supply to Rome, which transited from merchant ship to River Tiber there. Again, the legionaries bolstered other firefighting resources, particularly the *vigils urbani*.

## Agriculture and industry

Legionaries also played a key role in agricultural and industrial enterprises in the Roman Empire. Their experience of both is detailed here.

In the first instance, the legionaries needed to be fed, both when in camp and on campaign. Even in the case of the former, considerable effort was needed to supply the garrisoned troops. To that end the land around each permanent fortification was turned over to providing the supplies needed to feed the troops. This was a substantial task considering the large size of many Roman military formations (see Introduction for detail on the various types of permanent Roman fortification). The troops ate two set meals per day, the *prandium* breakfast and the *cena* evening meal.

When considering the permanent garrisons of the Roman military, it should be noted that the legionaries and other troop types did not live in isolation, but were always part of their own wider community. Many civilians lived alongside them, through both choice and obligation. When the military were stationed in their permanent bases such civilians (up to 200,000 by some calculations in Britain for example) most often resided in the surrounding *vicus* settlements (or *canabae* in the context of a legionary fortress). These featured all of the trades and supporting activities needed to maintain the regional military presence, including those engaged in agriculture. It is therefore likely that even if the legionaries were directly engaged in agriculture to provide their own subsistence (at the very least through its management), they would have been part of this wider community.

However, it was when on campaign that the Roman military machine really swung into action in terms of subsistence, it being crucial to ensure the troops were sustained well enough to be at their martial best. Provisioning was carried out through three types of base – supply bases provisioned by the provincial governor (for example South Shields, Cramond and Carpow in the context of the Severan campaigns in Scotland), operational bases and tactical bases. The latter were often the marching camps, and it was not uncommon for those not slighted after their initial use to be converted into supply depots, often becoming permanent fortifications in this capacity. Meals were taken in the marching camps again in the morning and evening, though with the latter taking priority given the usual necessity for an early start. The legionaries were required on campaign to carry three days' worth of rations – the nature of which depended on the location of the campaign – with the supplies requisitioned from the surrounding populace/countryside when the supply chain was stretched. The principal difference when on campaign to the diet in garrison seems to have been a switch in the use of the grain ration, from making bread to making the *bucellatum* army biscuit.

Meanwhile, in addition to engaging in agriculture for their own subsistence, the Roman state also deployed the legionaries to run agricultural imperial estates (land owned specifically by the emperor). These were particularly extensive in the eastern empire where they tracked crown land previously owned by earlier Hellenistic rulers. However, one of the better examples showing military involvement in the running of agricultural imperial estates is Stonea in the Fens in East Anglia, Britain. There is evidence here that after the Boudiccan revolt the region remained comparatively under-developed given the depopulation and economic turbulence after the rebellion. The state was therefore keen to use the military to set things on a satisfactory course, especially given much of the land (some poor quality) would have needed careful management to bring it up to an acceptable standard for profitable agriculture. The military then remained throughout the occupation, with evidence of such a presence including military belt fittings and silver and gilt crossbow-type brooches (the latter late Roman and often associated with the military).

Turning to industry, a responsibility particularly associated with the Roman legionary (and the military more broadly) was managing *metalla* enterprises. This is a catch-all Roman term for any form of extractive industry, for example quarrying and mining. In the Roman Empire such activity was often on an epic scale, and frequently in the context of industrial imperial estates. Given their importance to the economy, the state repeatedly turned to the military to ensure continuity of the supply of mined and quarried material from these enterprises.

*Severan land walls of London, section near Tower Hill tube station. Ragstone, sourced and transported from the upper Medway Valley by the Roman military who then built the wall.*

In south-east Britain there are two overt examples of the legionaries and military running such *metalla*. These were in upper Medway Valley and the Weald. In the upper Medway Valley there was an intensive ragstone quarrying industry where five enormous quarries upriver of the tidal reach provided much of the building stone for the region (particularly London) from around AD 50 through to the middle of the 3rd century AD. It has recently been argued that given the scale involved the legionaries (and military more broadly) would certainly have played a role here. Meanwhile in the Weald there was a widespread iron manufacturing industry making use of regionally mined iron ore, with the larger manufactories being located near the coast. This industry provided much of the iron needed for the Roman military in Britain for the same period of time as the nearby ragstone quarrying industry, though the key state presence here seems to have been the Classis Britannica regional fleet. However, legionaries would certainly have been involved, especially at the outset given each site needed to be surveyed to allow extractive operations to begin.

## Engineering and construction

Perhaps the best-known non-conflict role of the legionary was engineering and construction. The output of this expertise is evident across the empire, whether in the form of the Roman road network, canals and canalised rivers, bridges, aqueducts, fortifications, public buildings or the wider built environment. Such projects were facilitated by the military both at a grass roots level by individual soldiers, and also by legionary specialists.

The legionaries themselves were skilled engineers in their own right, with building and engineering playing an enormous part of their working life. To enable the warriors to fulfil such a roll, in addition to their panoply of fighting equipment each legionary in the late republic and Principate also carried a stake, saw, pickaxe, chain, sickle, basket and leather strap. When larger construction projects were undertaken by the legionaries it was common for manpower to be drawn from a variety of different units, for example the *vexillations* from legio II Augusta, legio VI Victrix and legio XX Valeria Victrix who all participated in the construction of Hadrian's Wall. Here, each legion was responsible for a specific stretch of wall construction. Such work entailed backbreaking hard physical labour. Experimental archaeology by the Royal School of Military Engineering in the UK has highlighted the sheer physicality of the work involved in road building, a common task for the legionary. They found it would have taken 40 man-hours to build 100 metres of roadway over grass, 450 man-hours to build the same distance over heathland and 600 man-hours, again for the same distance, through forest.

The legions of the later republic and Principate also included specialist pioneer military engineers, and also a large number of specialist craftsman, engineers and administrators attached to larger units, these including highly experienced surveyors, architects and builders. The pioneers fulfilled the same role as their counterparts in subsequent military formations throughout history. When on the march through enemy territory, these troops were tasked with forging ahead of the marching column to clear the path of the advance and, as the day's march neared its end, prepare for the construction of the marching camp. The legionaries then joined in the work as they arrived.

However it is the specialist legionaries who are of most interest here. Each legion contained a very wide range of artisan skills and crafts. The primary sources say these including ditch diggers, farriers, pilots, master builders, shipwrights, ballista makers, glaziers, arrow makers, bow makers, smiths, coppersmiths, helmet makers, wagon makers, roof-tile makers, water engineers, sword cutlers, trumpet makers, horn makers, plumbers, blacksmiths, masons, woodcutters, limeburners, charcoal burners, butchers, huntsmen, sacrificial animal keepers, grooms and tanners. All such specialist legionaries were dubbed *immunes* – soldiers exempted from general duties because of their skills.

*Monumental fortifications built by the legionaries of legio II Augusta. The walls of the* civitates *capital at Caerwent, south-east Wales.*

Additionally, the specialist military personnel in the legions also included *agrimensor* land surveyors, *librator* land levellers and *mensor* quantity measurers (and in the case of the military building aqueducts *aqualegus* aqueduct inspectors). These legionaries were the supreme surveyors of the ancient world, putting the stamp of Rome in a very physical way everywhere they went. Highly skilled professionals, they used a number of tools, instruments, and techniques to plan the settlements, farmland, courses for roads and aqueducts and fortifications that were an everyday part of living within the Roman Empire.

The legionary expertise in surveying was an amalgam of the experience gained or acquired as the republic, and later the Principate, expanded and integrated new cultures. Whether building roads of epic scale or creating new stone-built planned settlements (for example London, a Roman founding), the legionary *agrimensores*, *libratores* and *mensores* used a panoply of advanced technical equipment that ensured the quality and accuracy of the work.

The output of these specialist legionaries in terms of engineering and construction are too numerous to detail here, so I will choose one example to show all such specialists at their

Technical equipment used by specialist legionaries included:

- The *decempeda*, a graduated measuring rod of 10 Roman feet with iron or bronze caps at either end. This was the principal tool of the surveyor.
- The *groma*, a vertical staff with a tapered end. This featured at the top horizontal cross-pieces mounted at right angles onto a bracket. Each had a plumb line with bob attached hanging vertically from each end, the tool being used to survey straight lines and right angles.
- The *chorobates*, a Roman spirit level featuring a long wooden frame with vertical legs, plumb bobs, a water level in a channel carved in the top and sightlines to assist finding the true horizontal.
- The *dioptra*, a circular table fixed to a tripod calibrated with angles, originally invented in Greece. This was the forerunner of modern surveying equipment, used when even greater accuracy was required than that provided by the *chorabates*, or when a gradient was too steep to use the *groma*.
- The *libra*, a further means of measuring gradients, thought to be a set of scales with a sighting tube.
- The *hodometer*, an advanced tool for measuring distance. This consisted of a small cart which the surveyor would push along featuring a one-toothed gear that was attached to the cart wheel, this engaging another gear featuring 399 short teeth and one longer tooth. Once the cart had travelled a distance of one Roman mile the long tooth pushed a pebble into a bowl,

allowing the surveyor to count the distance travelled at the end of each day of surveying a new route.

working best. This is with regard to the legionary fortress that played such a key role in the life of the legionary. I use that at York to provide specific detail.

York is a Roman founding, owing its existence to the Roman conquest campaigns following the AD 43 invasion. Our protagonist here is the Cerialis we last saw in disgrace following the Boudiccan revolt. By AD 71 he was back in imperial favour following his recent putting down of the Batavian revolt of Julius Civilis in the Rhine Delta. As a reward he was made the governor of Britannia, tasked by Emperor Vespasian with securing the north from the local Brigantes tribe.

The primary sources say that Cerialis immediately headed north upon arrival, in the first instance ordering the veteran legio IX Hispana (with whom he had been disgraced in AD 60/61) out of its legionary fortress at Lincoln into Yorkshire where the troops constructed a new fortress on the northern bank at the point where they crossed the River Ouse. This was a particularly defensible position as the spot chosen was where the tributary River Foss runs into the Ouse, providing riverine protection on two flanks. It was here that the legionary *agrimensor* land surveyors, *librator* land levellers and *mensor* quantity measurers laid out the plan of the new fortress, using their *decempeda* measuring rods, *groma* sighting tools, *chorobates* spirit levels, *dioptra* circular measuring tables, *libra* measuring scales and *hodometer* distance measurers.

Once the site had been surveyed the construction specialists got to work. Here the master builders managed an operation featuring a wide range of their *immunes* colleagues, including masons, woodcutters, limeburners, charcoal burners, plumbers, blacksmiths, ditch diggers, roof-tile makers, water engineers and

*Detail of the Porta Nigra, Trier, showing later Roman elite military engineering skills.*

glaziers. Raw muscle was provided by the non-specialist legionaries in the legion, the *auxilia* and the local population. The legionaries, specialists and otherwise, used a wide variety of equipment in the primary construction phase. At the most basic these included:

- Ropes, made in a variety of different ways to create elasticity, allowing them to be used not only for binding and pulling but also as a spring to conserve energy.
- Pulleys, used to gear force.
- Winches, mounted either horizontally or vertically. In the case of the former they could be utilised by turning the outward spokes of a horizontally mounted wheel using men or oxen. For vertical winches, men only were used (though certainly not legionaries) to tread on the inside of the vertically positioned wheel.

The application of these basic units in various combinations allowed the creation of the wide variety of machinery used by the legionaries and others for construction projects. Such machinery included cranes and hoists to lift heavy materials to great heights, scaffolding, mills of all sizes to ground the raw materials to make mortar, trusses of ceramics or wood, and pile drivers to drive stakes and piles into the ground.

One good example of such technology is the tread wheel crane (called the *polyspaston* by the Romans), which used vertically mounted winch gearing. Of wooden construction, this crane was powered by men actually inside the tread wheel, with the ropes attached to a pulley system that turned onto a spindle through the rotation of the wheel, allowing the crane to hoist or lower very heavy loads. A fine example of such a crane is depicted on a tomb near the Porta Maggiore in Rome. This substantial lifting device is shown actually being built, featuring a two-sheave pulley. Meanwhile, if the load needing to be lifted was actually larger than the capacity of the tread wheel crane, a wooden lifting tower was built featuring a rectangular trestle designed such that the material needing to be lifted could be carried

*Basilica of Constantine, Trier. Almost certainly built by the Roman military.*

upright through the middle of the structure using human- or animal-powered capstans on the ground around the tower.

Back to York, the fortress was completed in short order. The scale of effort by legio IX Hispana in that regard is evident through analogy, with over 100,000 man-days estimated to have been needed to build the 760-metre wall circuit at the later Saxon Shore fort at Pevensey in East Sussex and 420,000 man-days for the Severan land walls of London. It was now that the other legionary *immunes* came into their own as they set up their operations to help facilitate the running of the legion. These included the farriers, pilots, shipwrights, ballista makers, arrow makers, bow makers, smiths, coppersmiths, helmet makers, wagon makers, sword cutlers, trumpet makers, horn makers, butchers, huntsmen, sacrificial animal keepers, grooms and tanners. The legio IX Hispana was soon at home and would stay until the early 2nd century when it was replaced by the legio VI Victrix around AD 120. An associated *canabae* town also developed opposite the new legionary fortress on the south bank of the river.

The original fortress on the site in York was classically playing card in shape and very large, enclosing an area of over 20 hectares and able to easily host the 5,000 or so men of the resident legion. Its original defences were a ditch and 3-metre-high turf/clay rampart topped by a palisade, together with wood-built towers and gates. From around AD 150 however the whole was replaced by a stone-built structure with a tile bonding layer, this a common design visible across the empire as far afield as the fortifications in London, Richborough, Rome and Constantinople. As the occupation progressed the defences increased in sophistication, ultimately featuring a string of defensive towers or bastions such as the multangular tower visible today next to the modern Yorkshire Museum in what would have been the west corner of the fortress.

**Legionary fortresses** had three uses:
- To provide accommodation for the men and equipment of its resident legion.
- To protect the legion if their base was attacked. The sophistication of the defences were designed from the outset to discourage such an eventuality.
- To act as a base for the legion and other military units to initially suppress and then conquer its enemies.

Inside the fortress at York, in all its iterations, was a grid pattern of streets and buildings, showing the sophistication of the surveying and construction expertise of the legionaries who originally built the site. The four corners were positioned at the points of the compass, facing north, south, east and west, hence the playing card shape. The principal streets within the fortress were called the *via principalis* (main street) and the *via praetorian*. The four *portae* gates to the fortress gave access to the main roads and still correlate with modern entrances to the city. One gave access to Ermine Street, the great northern road linking York with London, while another gave access to Dere Street, the road north into Scotland.

At the centre of the fortress, dividing the *via praetoria* and with the *via principalis* passing across its front, was the parade ground

*Multangular tower, York, part of the fortifications of the legionary fortress there, first occupied by legio IX Hispana and later legio VI Victrix.*

featuring the 'headquarters' *principia* building which housed the senior base commander and his staff. On one side of this parade ground, perpendicular to the *principia* itself, stood an associated *basilica* great aisled hall. The scale of the latter, certainly from the time of Septimius Severus' arrival when he made the town his imperial capital, was immense given the size of the single column recovered in 1969 during excavations of the structure. At 68 m long, 32 m wide and 23 m in height, this *basilica* would have stood just short of the modern height of today's York Minister. Such a size for the rebuilt *basilica* (the *principia* itself would similarly have been restyled at the time of Severus' stay) would certainly reflect the use of the legionary fortress and its extensive *canabae* as the imperial capital while Severus prepared for his assault on the north.

From the *principia* the legion at York was administered and its religious ceremonies performed, while it was from the *tribunal* podium at one end of the adjacent *basilica* that the commanding officer (and later Severus as emperor) would have addressed his troops and received visiting dignitaries. Meanwhile, in the *principia* itself a row of rooms would have served as offices, with the central one being the *aedes,* the legionary shrine and the spiritual heart

*Monumental column from the basilica attached to the* principia *of the Roman legionary fortress, York. Dates to the time of Septimius Severus when he turned the city into his imperial capital for the last three years of his life.*

*Site of the legionary fortress at Caerleon, south eastern Wales, home to the legio II Augusta. Barracks blocks and bread ovens in view.*

of the fortress. It was here that the legionary standards were kept. The *aedes* also had a more practical function in that beneath its floor sat a vault in which was kept the legionary pay chest. There is no doubt that, even before any Severan expansion, the *principia* with its grand *basilica* at the legionary fortress in York would have been astonishing to the people of the area, a true statement of the power of Rome in the furthest dark north-west of the empire. From the time of Severus it would have been even grander.

Other buildings in close proximity to the *principia* included the *praetorium*, the commanding officer's house, built in the same manner as a fine town house and used for business as well as domestic purposes. Meanwhile, also around the central parade ground (and again next to the *principia* to provide ease of access) was the building that housed the legionary supply officer. The rest of the fortress interior was packed out with a wide variety of buildings and structures, some stone-built and some wooden, set out in a regularised pattern such that any incumbent in the fortress would know as a matter of fact where every amenity was. Such buildings included a large number of barracks to house the troops, granaries to feed them, workshops to manufacture and maintain all of their equipment, a hospital and a bath house. The latter was

*Barracks building at the Roman fort, supply base and fortified harbour site at Cramond on the Firth of Forth.*

*Roman amphitheatre at the legionary fortress of Caerleon in south-east Wales, home to the legio II Augusta.*

a very important feature of the Roman cultural experience and served to remind many of the troops of their Mediterranean roots, at least early in the occupation. One can imagine how popular the bath house, with its piping-hot steam rooms, would have been in the heart of a northern British winter to the legionaries of legio IX Hispana and later legio VI Victrix. The actual legionary bath house at York was located in the southern corner of the fortress during excavations in 1972 which uncovered an associated Roman sewer, this helping identify that it occupied an area of 9,100 m².

A mystery surrounds one final key building associated with the Roman legionary fortress in York. This is its missing amphitheatre. These iconic Roman structures are often found in close proximity to fortifications of some kind. Examples in Britain include the fine amphitheatres at the legionary fortresses at Caerleon and Chester, and that at the *vexillation* fort at Cripplegate in London. However, one has yet to be found in York, although experts believe its remains to be there but obscured by the modern built environment.

One can see from the above description of this complex fortification in York that the legionaries played the key role at every step of its construction and use. These elite warriors were thus the reason it was built, the means by which it was constructed, its inhabitants and ultimately its defenders, providing a superb example of the legionary as an engineer and builder.

# CHAPTER 5

# OTHER ROMAN TROOP TYPES AND THE LATE ROMAN ARMY

The Roman legionary never fought in isolation and was always part of a complex military machine involving many other troop types. This was case throughout the republic, Principate and Dominate, and in differing ways for each time period. In this chapter I first consider the mercenaries and allies which bolstered the legionaries of the mid and later republic. I then detail the *auxilia* and regional fleets of the Principate, before looking at the later Roman army of the Dominate to show how the legionary changed over time.

## Mercenaries and allies of the mid and later republic

Given the limited diversity of the Camillan, Polybian and Marian legions, additional troops types were recruited as mercenaries and allies to fulfil supporting roles on the battlefield. These all fought in their own native fashion.

Early in the republic such troops were recruited from Italy. Examples included Latin neighbours, or the hill tribesmen of the Hernici, Aequi, Umbri, Sabini and Volsci. These were soon joined by warriors from Samnium and Magna Graecia. However, from this point as Rome began its irresistible advance across first the western and then eastern Mediterranean, the mercenaries and allies began to be recruited from much further afield. This was to have a dramatic effect not only on the make up of the mid and later republican armies, but also on the equipment of the legionaries themselves.

In its wars against Carthage the Romans first came up against troops from Gaul, Spain and North Africa. Impressed, they recruited them in large numbers. The Gauls were renowned for their fierce charge, their elite warriors wearing coats of mail and iron helmets which the legionaries began to adopt. Meanwhile the Spaniards, equally fierce, provided the inspiration for the *scutum*, *pilum* and *gladius*. Both also supplied the bulk of the cavalry used by the mid and later republican armies in the west. Meanwhile, from North Africa Rome recruited Numidian light horse, famous for skirmishing and armed with javelins with which they showered their foes. It was also from here that the later republican and early Principate Roman armies sourced their elephants.

To these troops, exotic and otherwise, the Romans added other specialist troop types in the western Mediterranean, particularly light infantry. These included javelinmen from Germany, Spain and Numidia, bowmen from across the region and slingers from Syracuse and the Balearic Isles, the latter particularly skilled with their weapon and much in demand as mercenaries.

Once Rome turned its attention to the Hellenistic kingdoms of the eastern Mediterranean even more troop types began to bolster the ranks of the legionary spearheads as they knocked out the successor kingdoms of Alexander and their neighbours one by one. The most ubiquitous were the Hellenistic *thureophoroi* who strengthened the legionary line-of-battle from the mid-3rd century BC. These were named after their oval *thureos* shield, a development of the Celtic infantry shield. This was smaller and less substantial than the hoplite's *hoplon* but was more flexible. Armed with long spear and javelin, though unarmoured except for a helmet, the *thureophoroi* were initially light troops equipped for close combat in a secondary role but whose flexibility saw them used more and more in front line combat.

Rome first encountered **war elephants** when fighting Carthage and later Numidia; they made a huge impression on contemporary audiences. Two different elephant types were used in a military context in the classical world. The first was the Indian variety first encountered by Alexander the Great in the early AD 320s in India. He was so impressed he created his own elephant corps, this becoming a key feature of many later Hellenistic armies. Meanwhile, the second type was the smaller African forest elephant used by Ptolemaic Egypt, Carthage and Numidia. These were initially sourced from the Horn of Africa after the Ptolemies were cut off from supplies of Indian elephants by the Syrian Wars with the Seleucid Empire. They proved easy to breed in captivity and their use quickly spread westwards through North Africa. The largest variety of elephant, the African bush type, was the untrainable for war.

Interestingly given the Roman propensity for assimilating the tactics, techniques and equipment of their opponents, in the republican period they never tried to adopt the pike which was the weapon most associated with Hellenistic armies. Phalanxes of pikemen 16 deep, wielding weapons up to 6 metres in length and with the pikes of the front five ranks set at the charge, were the hallmark of the armies of Macedonia, later Greece, the Seleucid Empire and Ptolemaic Egypt. Polybius, in his *Histories* (18.28–32), describes the imperviousness of this dense, bristling formation:

> … so long as the phalanx retains its characteristic form and strength nothing can withstand its charge or resist it face to face…we can easily picture the nature and the tremendous power of a charge by the whole phalanx, when it advances 16 deep with levelled pikes.

Yet when the legionaries faced the pike phalanx in the crucial battles of conquest in the region, for example at Cynoscephalae against Philip V's Macedonians in 197 BC, Magnesia against Antiochus III's Seleucids in 190 BC and Pydna against Perseus' Macedonians in 168 BC, they won every time. This was due to the inherent flexibility of the Camillan and Polybian manipular system which was better able to making use of tactical advantages. It is likely that this flexibility, which also reflected the Roman martial psyche, was the main reason the pike wasn't adopted by the legions of republican Rome. In fact the only (unsuccessful) attempts to arm legionaries with pikes would come much later with Emperors Caracalla and Severus Alexander in the 3rd century AD.

Back to the mid-late republic, Thracian peltasts were also popular as mercenaries, armed with the wicked-looking *rhomphia* two-handed cutting weapon, javelins, and protected by the wicker *pelta* shield. These were bolstered by other specialist troop types, for example bowmen from Crete and slingers from Rhodes.

Mercenary cavalry were sourced from across the eastern Mediterranean, the principal suppliers being Macedonia and Greece. These mounted troops were armed in a very different fashion to the warriors who had fought with Alexander and his immediate successors. The latter had been shock troops equipped with the *xyston* lance, charging the enemy battle line in wedge formation and often delivering the battle-winning blow. However, by the time Macedon faced the growing might of Rome from the beginning of the 3rd century BC, Hellenistic line-of-battle cavalry had diminished to a skirmishing force using light spears and javelins. These only engaged enemy cavalry in hand-to-hand combat when necessary. Such a change in role is often associated with the introduction of the large cavalry shield in the 3rd century BC. This followed Pyrrhus' campaigns in Italy where he was suitably impressed by their use. The Galatian invasion of Greece in 279 BC was another catalyst. The advent of these shields made using the long *xyston* problematic for cavalry using the saddle technology of the day, and certainly by the time they were employed by the legions of Rome mercenary cavalry from the region had a very secondary role, scouting and protecting flanks.

**Formal allies** fought most visibly with the legions in the eastern Mediterranean. Prominent examples included Rhodes, the Aitolian League from mountainous central Greece, the Galatians (eastern Gauls) and Bithynians from Asia Minor, Armenians from the southern Caucasus Mountains and Judeans from the Levant. However, the best known example is the Pergamene force of Eumenes II which formed the left wing of the Roman army at Magnesia in 190 BC. This played a crucial role in the overwhelming Roman victory over the Seleucids, including facing down a terrifying scythed chariot charge.

## Auxilia

As detailed in Chapter 2, Augustus, the first emperor of the Principate, was a great military reformer. One of the most evident examples was the formal creation of the *auxilia* as an integral part of the Roman military machine. Over time these troops gradually replaced the use of ad hoc mercenaries and allies to bolster the legions. *Auxilia*, both infantry and cavalry, were recruited from non-Roman citizens, often those recently conquered in the new provinces as the new empire expanded.

Though full line-of-battle troops, the *auxilia* were the junior partners to their legionary counterparts. From the later 1st century AD infantry were paid 100 *denarii*, and cavalry 200 *denarii* (those cavalry based on the wing of a battle formation were paid 333 *denarii*). Terms of service were similar to those of the legionaries after the later reforms of Augustus, this being 25 years. Upon retirement the trooper was given a citizenship diploma granting Roman citizenship to himself and his heirs, the right of legal marriage to a non-citizen woman, plus citizenship for existing children. There is no evidence that auxiliary veterans received any gratuity; and from AD 140 Antoninus Pius abolished the citizenship for children already born before discharge.

Despite their lower status when compared to the legionaries, *auxilia* were still a formidable fighting force and it was very rare for a campaigning army to comprise only legionaries (*auxilia* making up a significant component of the force Severus deployed for his *expeditio felicissima Brittannica* for example). Further, even when legionary forces were present, it was often only the *auxilia* who engaged in combat. A good example is provided by the battle of Mons Graupius in AD 83 when Agricola finally managed to bring the Caledonians to battle south of the Moray Firth in the Grampians during his attempt to conquer Scotland.

Infantry formations of the *auxilia* were based on a single *quingenary* cohort of 480 troops, or a double-sized *milliary* cohort of 800 troops. Auxiliary cavalry (which made up by far the largest mounted component of Principate military formations) were organised into *quingenary alae* of 512 men or *milliary alae* of 768. *Auxilia* units could also be fielded in units which featured both infantry and mounted troops, their organisation being less well understood. Such infantry cohorts, cavalry *alae* and combined units were very flexible and could easily be moved around the empire as needed in the same manner as *vexillations* of legionaries.

*Auxilia* infantry cohorts (both the small and large) were divided into centuries of between 80 and 100 men, these under the command of a centurion, clearly replicating the similar structure in a legionary formation. The centurions however, unlike the auxiliary troopers, were sometimes Roman citizens appointed from the legions (by the governor of a province or even directly by the emperor). Others were drawn direct from the rank and

*Roman* auxilia *in short chain mail hauberks on the Arch of Septimius Severus, Forum, Rome.*

file of the auxiliary unit. Above this level, the command of the overall cohort of *auxilia* was given over to equestrians, a *praefectus* for a *quingenary* unit and a *tribunus* for a *milliary* unit.

The majority of auxiliary foot troops were close order infantry who fought in a similar manner to the legionaries. They were armed with short, throwable spears called *lancea* rather than the specialised *pila* of the legionaries and a sword similar to the *gladius*. This was later replaced by the *spatha* as with the legionaries. *Auxilia* are never depicted in *lorica segmentata*, they most frequently being shown wearing chain mail or scale mail hauberks which were shorter and less sophisticated than the equivalents worn by their legionary counterparts. Their helmets seem to have been cheaper bronze versions of those worn by the legionaries, while auxiliary infantry shields are most often shown as an oval and flat design. Troops carrying this military panoply are certainly shown in epigraphy and sculpture, for example on Trajan's Column and the Arch of Septimius Severus in Rome.

The *auxilia* also provided most of the specialist troops of the Roman military formations, for example archers, slingers and javelinmen (later joined by staff slingers and even crossbowmen). The archers are particularly well represented in contemporary

*Roman legionary in* lorica segmentata *but with large oval body shield, Arch of Septimius Severus, Forum, Rome.*

epigraphy and sculpture, those on Trajan's Column showing a clear distinction between those originating in the east and those in the west. All appear to have been armed with the recurved composite bow. This advanced weapon was based around a wooden core onto which horn and animal sinews were carefully glued to create the recurved shape. The ends of the bow were then fitted with 'ears' protected by antler or bone. These acted as levers for the flexible limbs, with a lath on the grip used to stiffen the handle to prevent it bucking and flexing when the string returned after the release of an arrow.

Meanwhile, for most of the Principate, auxiliary cavalry seem to have been armed in a similar way to their infantry counterparts with chain mail shirts (shorter than those of the infantry to allow greater movement in the saddle, such armour weighing around 9 kilograms), with flat hexagonal or oval shields and spears (longer than those of their infantry counterparts). They also carried the *spatha* from a much earlier date and indeed it was from the auxiliary cavalry that the weapon's use was later transferred to the legionaries and foot *auxilia*. The armour and equipment of the auxiliary Roman cavalrymen did begin to change as the Principate progressed, becoming increasingly either heavier (ultimately as the *equites cataphractarii* and *clibanarii* of the later empire, see below) or specialised, for example the javelin-armed *equites illyriciani* and bow-armed *equites sagittarii* skirmishing light cavalry.

A final consideration regarding the *auxilia* is the fact that the individual units tended to maintain the cultural nuances of their place of origin. We have seen this above in Chapter 3, in the context of the Claudian invasion of Britain in AD 43 with the use of Batavians from the Rhine Delta to cross the River Medway downriver of the battle site there to flank the British forces and end the stalemate after the first day's fighting. These *auxilia* were renowned for their swimming ability in armour, though in this case they used inflated pigskins. Meanwhile, recent research into a possible insurrection of some kind in London during the Hadrianic period has argued that the many decapitated skulls found in the Wallbrook and its tributary streams dating to this period are the work of mounted auxiliaries exacting retribution against those challenging the rule of Rome. These troops, it is alleged, were head hunters in their homelands when fighting their enemies.

## The regional fleets

By the time of the Principate the naval power of Rome was manifest in independent, regional fleets. These had their origins once again with the Augustan reforms of the Roman military. Before this time the fleets of the republic were more often than not ad hoc in nature, designed to fight symmetrical engagements against opponents such as Carthage, the Hellenistic kingdoms or civil war rivals in the Mediterranean. As with many other aspects of Roman military power however, the fleets were professionalised under Rome's first emperor, their regional basis reflecting the empire's expanding geographical reach. By the end of the 1st century AD there were 10 such regional fleets, each with a very specific area of territorial responsibility.

To give a flavour of the ubiquity of the *auxilia*, the below table details the origins and location of many auxiliary cohorts and *alae* found in the provinces in the later 2nd and 3rd centuries AD.

| Unit | Location | Date |
|---|---|---|
| Brittones Aurelianensis | Upper Germany | AD 200 |
| Cohors Sagittariorum | Hispania Baetica | Later 2nd century AD |
| Cohors I Aelia Brittonum milliaria | Noricum | Later 2nd century AD |
| Cohors I Aelia Dacorum millaria | Britannia and Noricum | Later 2nd/early 3rd century AD |
| Cohors I Dardanorum Aurelia | Dalmatia | Later 2nd century AD |
| Cohors I Delmatorum | Dalmatia | Later 2nd century AD |
| Cohors I Frisavonum | Britannia | Later 2nd/3rd century AD |
| Cohors I Hemesenorum eq. mil. Sagittaria CR | Pannonia Inferior | Later 2nd century AD |
| Cohors I Pasinatum Aurelia Nova | Dalmatia | Later 2nd century AD |
| Cohors I Sacorum Aurelia Nova | Dalmatia | Later 2nd century AD |
| Cohors I Septima Belgarum | Upper Germany | AD 200 |
| Cohors I Ulpia Tiaiana Cugernorum CR | Britannia | 2nd/3rd centuries AD |
| Cohors I Ulpia Traiana Campestris Voluntariorum | Dalmatia | 2nd/3rd centuries AD |
| Cohors II Aforum Flavia | Mauretania | Late 2nd century AD |
| Cohors II Astorum Equitata | Britannia | 2nd/3rd centuries AD |
| Cohors II Dacorum Aurelia | Pannonia Inferior | Late 2nd century AD |
| Cohors II Gallorum Equitata | Britannia | 2nd/3rd centuries AD |
| Cohors III Aquitanorum equitata CR | Upper Germany | Late 2nd century AD |
| Cohors III Gallorum | Hispania Baetica | Late 2nd century AD |

| Unit | Location | Date |
|---|---|---|
| Cohors III Nerviorum CR | Britannia, Hispania Baetica | Late 2nd century AD |
| Cohors III Breucorum | Britannia | 2nd/3rd centuries AD |
| Cohors III Tungorum mil. | Mauretania | Late 2nd century AD |
| Cohors V Baetica | Hispania Baetica | Late 2nd century AD |
| Cohors V Gallorum | Britannia | Early 3rd century AD |
| Cohors VI Raetorum | Britannia | Late 2nd century AD |
| Cohors VII Delmatorum eq. | Mauretania | Late 2nd century AD |
| Ara Colonia Ulpia Traiana | Lower Germany | Late 2nd century AD |
| Ala Asturum | Gallia Lugdunensis | 2nd/3rd centuries AD |
| Ala (Gallorum) Placentia | Britannia | Late 2nd century AD |
| Ala (Hispanorum) Vettonum CR | Britannia | 2nd/3rd centuries AD |
| Ala Noricorum | Lower Germany | Late 2nd century AD |
| Ala (Gallorum) Sebosiana | Britannia | 2nd/3rd centuries AD |
| Ala I (Hispanorum) Aravacorum | Pannonia | Late 2nd century AD |
| Ala I Asturum | Britannia | 2nd/3rd centuries AD |
| Ala I Britannica | Mauretania | Late 2nd century AD |
| Ala I Caninafatium | Pannonia | Late 2nd century AD |
| Ala I Contaforium | Pannonia | Late 2nd century AD |
| Ala I Ituraeorum | Pannonia | Late 2nd century AD |
| Ala I (Pannoniourum) Sebosiana | Britannia | 2nd/3rd centuries AD |
| Ala I (Pannoniorum) Tampiana | Britannia | Later 2nd century AD |
| Ala II Asturum | Britannia | 2nd/3rd centuries AD |
| Ala II Pannoniorum | Pannonia | 2nd/3rd centuries AD |

After D'Amato, R. 2016. *Roman Army Units in the Western Provinces (1)*. Oxford: Osprey Publishing, p. 14

To give specific detail on the regional fleets I turn to Britain once more, with the Classis Britannica, Britain's first ever navy. The manpower complement of this fleet and its 900 ships can be inferred from the size of the wider Roman fleet, and its regional components, over time. The original Roman war fleets created to fight the First and Second Punic Wars were extensive, given the nature of the conflict across the western Mediterranean, numbering up to 60,000 men in terms of crew for the second iteration. Most of these would have been rowers, for example 30,000 such specialists being needed for the 203 BC invasion of Africa to man 160 warships. This 60,000 overall figure would have fallen to around 30,000 by the reign of Augustus at the end of the 1st century BC, then rising to around 50,000 again by the reign of Hadrian in the 2nd century AD as the regional fleets reached maturity. Key factors in this increase over 120 or so years would have been the growth of the Classis Germanica (incorporated very late in the 1st century BC) and creation of the Classis Britannica in the later 1st century AD. The British fleet had its origins in the abandoned Caligulan invasion of Britain and the actual Claudian invasion, but was first called this title in the context of the Batavian Revolt of Julius Civilis in AD 70. As can be seen above, based on the stipend paid to their commanders, these two sister fleets were jointly the third most important fleets in the empire after the Italy-based Classis Misenensis and Classis Ravennas. It is from the complements of these two latter fleets that we can start to infer the size of the Classis Britannica. During the reigns of Otho and Vitellius in AD 69 the former had a complement of 6,000 and the latter 10,000 (this calculation based on the number of marines and sailors converted for legionary land-based warfare during the civil war of that year). One can then cross-reference these figures with the military mission of the Classis Britannica, which would have needed at least three large squadrons to fulfil the various roles detailed below; and the known Classis Britannica bases at Boulogne where the fort would have accommodated 3,500, Dover (640 men) and other bases such as Richborough, Lympne

## Regional Fleets of the Roman Principate

The 10 regional fleets in existence at the end of the 1st century AD. The size of the annual stipend for each fleet's commander gives an indication of their seniority in the wider military framework of the empire.

| Fleet | Annual stipend |
|---|---|
| Classis Ravennas | 300,000 sesterces |
| Classis Misenensis | 200,000 sesterces |
| Classis Britannica | 100,000 sesterces |
| Classis Germanica | 100,000 sesterces |
| Classis Pannonica | 60,000 sesterces |
| Classis Moesica | 60,000 sesterces |
| Classis Pontica | 60,000 sesterces |
| Classis Syriaca | 60,000 sesterces |
| Classis Nova Libica | 60,000 sesterces |
| Classis Alexandrina | 60,000 sesterces |

Ellis Jones, J. 2012. *The Maritime Landscape of Roman Britain.* Oxford: BAR/Archaeological and Historical Associates Ltd, p. 61.

and Pevensey (the latter two both presumed to have featured Classis Britannica forts). Based on all of these factors it has been calculated that the complement of the Classis Britannica would have been around 7,000 men.

Command of the fleets was also reformed under Augustus, he doing away with the single naval command structure of the republic that had been led by a single consular-level officer, perhaps with a *praetor* commander from the army beneath him. Instead, to provide greater flexibility, this arrangement was replaced in the regional fleets with a devolved structure featuring an equestrian-level *praefectus classis* who was appointed directly by the emperor for each individual fleet. He reported to the province's procurator rather than the governor, although clearly falling under the latter's command for military operations. Commanding the regional fleet was an important post, with the *praefectus Classis Britannicae* being third only to the governor and procurator in terms of importance within the province's military and civilian chains of command. As the Principate progressed the post grew in importance even more. The holder was initially a senior former legionary or auxiliary officer, with epigraphic evidence suggesting that it was common for the *praefectus classis* to switch between land-based military and naval command, and also between both of these and senior civilian posts. Later in the 1st century AD, as part of Claudius' rationalisation of the civil and military branches of the administration of the empire, the role of the *praefectus classis* was opened up to allow freedmen of the imperial household to hold the post. This changed back following the 'Year of Four Emperors' in AD 69 when sea power played a key role in the eventual victory of Vespasian, the post once again being reserved for members of the equestrian class.

As part of his headquarters organisation, the *praefectus classis* had a specialist staff to help manage his regional fleet. This featured his second-in-command, called the *subpraefectus* (an aide-de-camp and executive officer), together with a *cornicularius* acting as third in command and chief of staff. Other key members of the team included *beneficiarii* posted from the governor's *officium consularis*, *actuarii* (clerks), *scribae* (writers) and *dupliarii* (leading ratings) attached from the naval component of the fleet.

Below the headquarters staff, the hierarchy of the regional fleets relied heavily on Hellenistic nomenclature, adapted following Rome's contact with the Greek world in the mid and later republic. Thus the commander of a squadron of ships was called the *navarchus* (the most senior being called the *navarchus principes*), with the captain of an individual vessel being called a *trierarchus* (this referencing the name's origins with the commander of a trireme). As the hierarchy progressed downwards, land-based Roman military nomenclature was added, with the *trierarchus'* executive team including the *gubernator* (the senior officer who was responsible for the steering oars), the *proretus* second lieutenant and the *pausarius* rowing master. Other junior officers on the staff of the *trierarchus'* included the *secutor* (master at arms), some *nauphylax* officers of the watch and specialists such as the *velarii* (with responsibility for the sails) and the *fabri* ships' carpenters.

The ship's company itself, below the level of the executive team, was called a century, reflecting the preference of the republican Roman navies for close action based on the expertise of their legionary and *auxilia* land-based counterparts. The century was commanded by a centurion, again a direct transference of terminology from the legions, who was assisted by his own team which comprised an *optio* second in command, a *suboptio* junior assistant, a *bucinator* bugler or *cornicern* horn player, and finally an *armorum custos* armourer.

The rest of the ship's complement comprised marines (*ballistarii* artillery crew, *sagittarii* archers and *propugnatores* deck soldiers), *velarius* sailors, and plenty of *remiges* oarsmen (always professionals, not slaves as depicted in popular culture), the whole company being styled *milites* (soldiers, the singular being *miles*) as opposed to *nautae* sailors, again reflecting the original republican preference for maritime close action.

At the beginning of the Principate, service as a naval *miles* was less well regarded than serving as a legionary or *auxilia*, although this did change over time as the regional fleets began to make their presence felt. The initial recruits for the navies came from local communities with maritime experience in each fleet's area of responsibility. This recruiting base expanded as the empire grew, and by the 2nd century recruits were being sourced from communities further afield. The terms of service for all of the ranks in the regional navies (up to the *trierarchus*) was 26 years, this then being rewarded with Roman citizenship. Only the *navarchus* could achieve citizenship within this 26-year service period. Perhaps reflecting recruitment issues, after AD 160 this term of service was increased to 28 years.

Each naval *miles* received three gold pieces or 75 *denarii* upon enlistment, with basic annual pay at the onset of the Principate for the lower ranks being 100 *denarii*, putting them on a similar level to the *auxilia*. Crew members with greater responsibilities were paid an additional amount on top of this, for example those being paid 1.5 times the normal salary being called *sesquiplicarii* and those being paid twice the amount being called *duplicarii*.

The actual vessel types utilised by the regional fleets differed chronologically and geographically during the Principate, although by this time the ram and ballista-equipped *liburnian* bireme war galley had by and large replaced the giant polyremes of the mid and late republic. The regional fleets also utilised a variety of different *myoparo* and *scapha* cutters and skiffs, and transport vessels of all types. An interesting point of interest here, specifically regarding the *liburnae*, is that they seem to have been individually named. An example is provided by the grave stele of a junior officer of the Classis Ravennate which describes him as the captain of the *liburna Aurata* (*Golden*). As recently determined, the regional fleets of this period had specific military roles, these being: blue-ocean sea control of the regional oceanic zone; control of the coastal littoral zone in the region of responsibility (littoral being waters in sight of the coast); intelligence gathering and patrolling; transport, supply and amphibious warfare; general maritime supply; and communications.

The regional fleets also fulfilled a variety of civilian functions, in effect being the equivalent of a modern army service corps. In so doing it contributed to the similar activities of the legions. The most glamorous role for the naval *milites* in this regard was to help facilitate the smooth running of the games in the arenas of the empire, particularly around the Mediterranean and in the east. This was with regard to their use in operating the *vela* (sail) awnings in arenas such as the Colosseum in Rome, which provided vital shade against the hot sun. Here permanent detachments from the Classis Ravennate and Classis Misinensis were stationed for this purpose. However, such a role may occasionally have been slightly less savoury, with Commodus known to have called on these sailors to punish the crowd on occasion, emphasising that even when deployed within a civilian context the military were still 'other' when compared to the rest of society.

Clothing for the naval *milites* differed between the regional fleets, reflecting differing climatic and operational conditions. Taking the Classis Britannica as an example again, an essential item of clothing in the northern waters at the edge of empire would have been the *birrus* rain-proofed woollen hooded cloak. This was an item of clothing for which Britain was famous across the empire. Other key clothing items would have been the *pilos* conical felt hat, a belted tunic with trousers, and either sandals or felt stockings with low-cut leather boots rather than the legionary *caligae*. The short *sagum* would have been worn when on formal duty.

For weaponry the marines of the regional navies were armed and equipped in a similar fashion to land-based auxiliaries. The principal missile weapons, in addition to artillery, would have been the bow, sling, javelin and dart. *Pila* armour-penetrating javelins as used by the legionaries would also have been utilised at close range, while for hand-to-hand work the marines would have been armed with boarding pikes, the *hasta navalis* naval spear, various types of sword and the *dolabra* boarding axe. Armour would again mirror that of the *auxilia*, with a hip-length shirt of chain mail or scales, while in sculpture the *navarchus* and *trierarchus* are often depicted wearing a muscled cuirass. Helmets ranged from those of a standard military pattern made at state-run *fabricae* to simple conical types. Finally, for a shield the marines used the auxiliary wood and leather oval design which, when at sea, would have been stowed along the sides of the *liburnae* over the oar ports.

Two examples from Britain show the regional fleets in action, and how they interacted with the legions and *auxilia*: Vespasian's lightning campaigns to conquer south-west Britain after the AD 43 Claudian invasion, and the Severan campaigns to conquer Scotland in the early 3rd century AD.

Vespasian was the legate of the legio II Augusta, which played a key role during Plautius' campaigns in AD 43. From AD 44 he was tasked with the subjugation of south-west Britain where the tribes were still notably hostile. The Roman historian Suetonius in his *The Twelve Caesars* (Vespasian 4) goes into great detail here, saying that the future emperor:

> … fought 30 battles, subjugated two warlike tribes (the Durotriges and Dumnonii), captured more than 20 oppida (fortified native urban centres), and took the Isle of White.

Vespasian's westward route was just inland from the coast, specifically to allow the fleet to provide close support. In this regard it would have secured his left flank in the littoral coastal zone to prevent the native Britons outflanking him by sea, and would of course have fulfilled the transport role for the campaign, carrying out all of the logistical heavy lifting to enable him to jump from objective to objective with ease. The fleet would also have provided intelligence gathering, its patrols giving advance notice of any British resistance well ahead of it being encountered.

As each natural harbour was approached by the landward forces in this pre-modern legionary *blitzkrieg* the fleet would have carried out an amphibious operation to secure the anchorage, with analogy from elsewhere in the empire showing legionaries, auxiliaries or even the fleet's own *milites* being used to carry out the task. These front-line harbours would then have been used as store bases to facilitate the quick supply of Vespasian's legionary spearheads, not only enabling rapid progress but building a strong supporting logistics chain behind the advance to maintain momentum. An extreme example of this, and also of the flank-securing function of the fleet, was the capture of the Isle of White early in Vespasian's campaign.

Evidence for the establishment of these regional 'assault' anchorages along the south coast has been found at a number of sites, for example at Bitterne at the head of Southampton Water.

Supporting archaeological data comes in the form of Claudian pottery, and more recently with the finding of large-scale Claudian-period storage buildings on the site of the later Roman settlement of Clausentum (today a suburb of Southampton) which sits at the tip of the Bitterne peninsula. From this location the goods arriving via the regional fleet in its transport role would have been ideally placed for forward deployment up the River Itchen to the advancing army.

Vespasian's progress can today be tracked by these coastal sites that he established during his westward progression. The next step from Bitterne can be found at Wimbourne in Dorset where he built an early *vexillation* fortress with an associated port and storage facility (this time on Poole Harbour). Weymouth Bay would then have been the location of the next fleet base given its proximity to the major military engagement site at Maiden Castle, where Vespasian's legionaries famously stormed the extensive hill fort defended by the Durotriges. Then heading deep into Dumnonian territory, a key fleet base was established at Topsham, immediately to the south of the later legionary fortress and *civitas* capital of Exeter (Roman Isca Dumnoniorum, of which it became the port).

After three seasons of campaigning, using this combination of land-based shock formations supplied and maintained by a series of new harbours built to keep pace with the legionary advance, the south-west was subdued. The British fleet, largely deployed to support Vespasian's campaigning in the region, would by this point have been strung out along the south coast to maintain the new anchorages with their extensive wharfs and storage facilities. The war galleys would also by now have been forging up into the Bristol Channel and Irish Sea, a brand new environment where they began scouting the coasts of Wales and Ireland to take control of the littoral zone there. A maritime threat from those directions was clearly evident, with the early fort built at Kingsholm, military harbours at Bridgewater, Sea Mills (Roman Portus Abonae) and Barnstable, and signal stations at Old Burrow, Martinhoe, Morwenstow and St Gennys evidence of this. The strategy and tactics used by Vespasian in his campaigns across the region, with the legionaries, *auxilia* and regional fleet acting in unison, was remarkably effective and by AD 47 his task was complete, he returning to Rome with Plautius.

By the time the warrior emperor Septimius Severus campaigned in Scotland the Classis Britannica was a mature force with 150 years of action to its name. As detailed in Chapter 3, its key military role in the AD 209 and AD 210 incursions north of the frontier was to seal off the coastal regions of the mid and upper Midland Valley up to the point where the Highland line met the North Sea around Stonehaven, and perhaps even further north up to the Moray Firth. As such the Maeatae and Caledonians (at least those in the mid and upper Midland Valley) would have been completely trapped in this lowland region by Caracalla's legionary spearhead driving north eastwards along the Highland line and the Classis Britannica along the coast. However this broad role can be unpacked into distinct activities which track the roles of the regional fleet set out above.

In the first instance, the fleet would have carried out the vital transport and supply roles, using the forts, supply bases and fortified harbours at South Shields on the Tyne, Cramond on the Forth and Carpow on the Tay. However, it is with regard to its combat roles in the Severan campaigns that we have clear sight of the regional fleet in military action. The principal combat roles of the Classis Britannica in these campaigns would have been littoral control (of both the coast and along the river networks), and also scouting, patrolling and reconnaissance. There would have been no requirement for activity in the oceanic blue water zone given the lack of any symmetrical threat, and the desire of any pre-modern navy to operate within sight of the coast if possible.

Littoral naval action differs in number of ways from open ocean warfare, with most military activity there tactical in nature, with decentralised command and control being the key to success given the rapidity with which a tactical and operational situation can change. Naval military operations in the littoral zone also required a different mix of platforms and capabilities than those required in the oceanic zone, and to this end the platforms available to the Classis Britannica during the Severan campaigns would have been ideal, specifically the fast and nimble *liburnae* bireme war galleys, *myoparo* cutters and *scapha* skiffs. All three types would have been ideal platforms with which to engage enemy forces in the littoral zone along the Scottish east coast, where they would have carried out coastal raiding to degrade the regional economies of the native Maeatae and Caledonians. The specific characteristics of carrying out military operations in the littoral zone include restricted space for manoeuvring (one should note here how many naval battles in the pre-modern era took place because one side was trapped against the coastline, for example the key naval battles of Carteia and the Ebro River in the Second Punic War), the dangerous marine environment for warships along a given coastline (when a sudden change in the weather could prove fatal, as evidenced by the loss of 27 Roman warships off Cape Palinuro in south-eastern Italy in AD 254 in the First Punic War), and the inherent difficulty in staying undetected by the enemy given the proximity of the coast and the associated reduction in warning time to respond to enemy aggression. For an excellent example of the latter we can look to the battle of Lilybaeum in 217 BC in the Second Punic War again, when a tip-off from Hiero of Syracuse led to the Roman interception of a Carthaginian naval raiding force and the capture of seven ships and 1,700 prisoners. However, it may well be that during the Severan campaigns in Scotland one of the desired outcomes was actually the opposite of this, the aim here being for the native Britons of the far north to actually see the might of the navy in action to damage local morale. We certainly have references to this during Agricola's late 1st century AD activities in the same region courtesy of the historian Tacitus.

The regional fleet would also have provided direct support to the ground forces by deploying up the navigable sections of the regional river systems, for example the Tay. Additionally, along the coast itself, the fleet would have forged ahead of the ground troops to seize any natural harbours and build fortified supply bases to ensure that as the legionaries and *auxilia* arrived along this coastal route provisions were available to maintain the lightning campaign speed the following day (replicating Vespasian's tactics in south-west Britain). The presence of the regional fleet would have also ensured that the native Britons had no chance whatsoever to mount any maritime raids to the coastal flank and rear of the advancing Roman land forces.

The Classis Britannica also provided the vital scouting, patrolling and reconnaissance functions to support the land campaign. Given its mix of vessel types and capabilities as set out above, it was ideally set to provide the military advancing in Scotland along its two axes with intelligence about what to expect along the line of advance in waters it knew very well. In that regard one can imagine the Classis Britannica being the eyes and ears of the advancing legionary spearheads on the maritime flanks of the army, whether along the coast or down the major river networks. The fleet's hard work was clearly noticed by Severus and Caracalla given coins featuring both Neptune and Oceanus were minted in AD 209 and have been interpreted as referencing the activity of the Classis Britannica. Further, some silver and bronze coins minted between AD 208 and AD 210 show a galley with its stern adorned with standards, as previously used on imagery dating to Trajan's Dacian campaigns.

The Severan campaigns detailed above were to prove the swansong for the Classis Britannica, and indeed the other regional fleets. It is last mentioned in an epigraphic funerary reference from Arles in southern France dated to AD 249. This references one Saturninus, a North African known to have been a *trierarchus* of the Classis Britannica. After this time the regional fleet disappears from history, perhaps a victim of the economic slump during the 'crisis of the 3rd century'. It was soon missed.

*Burgh Castle, Norfolk. A Saxon Shore fort built by the Roman military.*

This is evident in the chain of expensive Saxon Shore forts that appeared in the south and east of Britain from this time (new research also showing others were built on the west coast), and with the appointment in AD 286 of the future usurper Carausius to clear the North Sea of endemic pirate raiding (unthinkable when the regional fleet existed).

## The later Roman army

The Roman Principate army most familiar to the general reader had begun a process of change during the reign of Septimius Severus between AD 193 and AD 211. Before this time, broadly, most Roman legions and *auxilia* units were based within easy reach of the borders of the empire. However, Severus created what could be termed the first Roman field army for his *expeditio felicissima Brittannica,* built around a core of his new legio II Parthica (which he based near Rome), the Praetorian Guard and the guard cavalry. To these he added the three British legions and many *vexillations* from the Rhine and Danube legions and auxiliary units until he was ultimately able to field an enormous land force of 50,000 men.

*Late Roman infantry group, note the* lorica hamata *chain mail and round oval body shield have replaced the Principate* lorica segmentata *and rectangular* scutum. *(Andy Singleton)*

This set a trend, accelerated by the challenges of the 'crisis of the 3rd century', with further major reforms being carried out by Diocletian and Constantine, such that the Dominate Roman military of the 4th century AD and onwards was very different to that of the Principate. The key changes included:

- A general levelling of the difference between the legionaries and auxiliaries in terms of standing, equipment and roles.
- Military units in general being smaller (sometimes much smaller), with an emphasis on creating brigades of troop types appropriate to a given task rather than having a single type of homogenous force.
- A clear distinction between *comitatenses* field army troops and *limitanei* border troops. This followed the adoption of a defence-in-depth strategy as the imperial experience changed from offence to defence, with the latter acting in a policing and 'trip wire' role on the borders of the empire and the former deployed far back to counter any significant incursion into imperial territory.
- A much larger mounted component within the field armies, with a greater range of specialist types.
- The disappearance of the Principate regional fleets (as detailed above), with a reversion to the republican concept of ad hoc fleets being created as required.
- Again reflecting earlier republican practice, the increasingly widespread use of *foederate* troops recruited from the Germans and Goths, armed in their own fashion but under Roman officers (and later under their own officers, these latter effectively mercenaries).

*Comitatenses* field army troops formed the battle line of the later Roman armies. The term (indicating such troops were at the emperor's immediate disposal) is first recorded in AD 325, by which time three principal regional field armies are detailed, two in the west (in Gaul facing the Rhine and Illyria the Danube) and one in the east. These had increased in number dramatically by

*Detail of later Roman legionaries with large oval body shields on the Arch of Constantine.*

the time of Theodosius (AD 379–395) who was able to deploy five field armies in the east alone, and more in the west. The field armies were commanded by a *magister equitum* (for the horse) and a *magister peditum* (for the foot), with a *magister militum* being appointed above them by the emperor when a particularly large force was assembled. Just as in the Principate with its *vexillations*, smaller units of *comitatenses* could also be brigaded together for specific roles (see above). These were commanded by a *comes*, a good example here being the force comprising four units sent to Britain in AD 367 under the *comes* Flavius Theodosius to counter the 'Great Conspiracy' of Picts, Attecotti, Irish and Germanic raiders who were overwhelming the frontier defences in the *diocese*.

As can be seen in Julian's order of battle at Strasbourg in AD 357, the legions and *auxilia* were by this time virtually identical in composition and equipment. Thus in his front line he fielded the Moesiaci, Pannoniaci, Iovani and Herculiani legions, flanked by elite auxiliaries units now called the *auxilia palatina* (the specific units at Strasbourg were the Petulantes, Heruli, Cornuti and Brachiati). In his second line he deployed the Primani legion, flanked by more *auxilia palatina* troops from the Celtae, Batavi and Regae units. It is probable all of these formations numbered only 1,000 or fewer, a far cry from the 5,000-man legions of the Principate.

*Late Roman infantry command group, with* lorica hamata *chain mail hauberks and oval body shields. Note the draco standard.*

The legionaries and *auxilia* were all armed with the long spear and *spatha,* with many also equipped with javelins and *plumbatae* or *martiobarbuli* lead weighted darts. These latter were carried in clips on the back of their large oval body shields and could be thrown over-arm for distance or under-arm to give a steep trajectory designed to fall on the heads of the approaching enemy. Armour was most frequently the long mail hauberk, while sophisticated helmets were now worn giving a very high degree of protection. The legionaries and *auxilia* armed and armoured in this fashion fought in deep formations, often with integral bowmen forming the rear ranks to fire over the heads of those in front. These troops were to be long-lived in their existence, particularly in the eastern empire after the fall of the western half in AD 476 with the abdication of Romulus Augustulus at the behest of his *magister militum* Flavius Odaocer. The armies of the Byzantine Empire (as the later eastern Roman Empire is known), though always including a very significant mounted component, were based around a core of such spear-armed foot soldiers called *skutatoi* after their shields. This was the ultimate evolution of the legionary, these troops continuing to exist into the 11th century AD.

*Captured Dacian and Sarmatian armour depicted on the base of Trajan's column. Such designs certainly had an influence on later Roman infantry armour.*

Meanwhile cavalry units still largely comprised *equites* reminiscent of the old auxiliary cavalry, though by this time many specialised types were also available in the field armies. These included *equites cataphractarii* and *clibanarii* troops in full armour and on fully or partially armoured horses, and javelin-armed *equites illyriciani* and bow-armed *equites sagittarii* skirmishing specialists.

One key difference for these *comitatenses* field army troops when compared to their Principate forebears was that they weren't based in permanent legionary fortresses. When not on active service they were instead billeted among local populations. Another observation is with regard to the élan of the *comitatenses* troops of the later field armies. There is no doubt that some of the military formations did retain their sense of martial elitism late into the empire, with for example the Iovani and Herculiani legions deployed by Julian at Strasbourg being particularly well regarded. These had previously been the legio V Iovia and legio VI Herculia, both foundings of Diocletian who later gave them their singular names when he turned them into his personal bodyguard.

However what is also evident is the difficulty experienced recruiting troops for many of the later legionary and auxiliary formations. Diocletian was forced to introduce a system whereby the sons of serving soldiers followed their fathers into their units, while Emperor Valentinian I (AD 364–375) reduced the height requirement of his legionaries from 1.8 m to 1.7 m. The primary sources also indicate that by this time many of those liable to be called to arms were deliberately mutilating themselves to be excused imperial service. Clearly gone was the swagger of the legions of Marius, Caesar, Augustus, Trajan and Severus.

The *limitanei* were a totally different fighting force. These troops were located on the frontiers of the empire in permanent bases, often the old border fortresses and forts of the Principate. Here they were based with their families who lived in the associated *canabae* or *vicus* settlements. Their role, as detailed above, was to act as a localised policing force in times of peace, and a trip wire when major incursions occurred. They were tasked in the latter case with buying time for the local *comitatenses* field army to arrive. This was often at great personal cost, for example the *limitanei* in Gaul who were destroyed by the raiding Alamanni prior to Julian's arrival. One can only guess the fate of their families.

Certainly early in the Dominate, the *limitanei* were equipped in a similar manner to less well-armed *comitatenses* field army troops. While few wore armour, most of the foot had helmets and carried the round oval body shield. For a weapon the short spear was used, together with the *spatha*. Mounted troops were equipped in a similar manner to the *comitatenses equites illyriciani* and *equites sagittarii*. Some units of *limitanei* could be attached to a field army in times of great crisis, in so doing earning the title *pseudocomitatenses*. As the Dominate progressed however, particularly in the west, the quality of the *limitanei* fell, and they should be regarded more as a local genderarmie from the beginning of the 5th century AD.

Finally in this consideration of the later Roman military, *foederates* increasingly made up a sizeable portion of the late Roman field armies, especially into the 5th century AD. The term originates from the word *foederatus* used to designate neighbouring states of the empire who provided military service in return for benefits and payment. It later extended in usage to cover the late Roman practice of subsidising entire barbarian confederations such as the Franks, Vandals, Huns and Visigoths. As set out above, while fighting in their own manner, *foederates* initially served under Roman officers. This changed as the empire in the west began its terminal decline, with whole bands of *foederate* warriors being hired en masse under their own leaders. It is in this context that we first meet the great Gothic leader Alaric, leading his own band of *foederate* Goths in Roman service. The first sight of this later development dates again to Julian who in AD 358, after his success at Strasbourg, made the entire Frankish confederation *foederates* in return for maintaining the Rhine border in northern Gaul. Similarly,

Emperor Valens in AD 376 allowed Fritigern's Goths to settle on the southern bank of the River Danube as *foederates*, and it is their mistreatment by the regional local government that prompted the uprising that saw the emperor and his combined eastern field armies destroyed at the crucial battle of Adrianople. Moving into the 5th century AD, *foederates* made up the bulk of the army of the *magister miletum* Flavius Aetius that defeated Attila the Hun at the battle of the Catalaunian Plains in AD 451. Significantly, this army also included a large number of allied troops, outside of the context of the *comitatenses* field army, showing the legions of Rome going full circle back to their republican roots in relying on non-Romans to fill out the line of battle and provide specialist troops.

# CONCLUSION

In this extensive review of the Roman legionary we have seen this elite warrior up close and personal. In the first instance he was a brutally efficient soldier, imbued for much of the history of the republic and empire with a deep sense of martial valour. Always ready to serve the emperor across the whole geographical diversity of the empire, the legionary was the tip of the Roman military spear during the early years of Imperial expansion, and later the bulwark upon which crashed *barbaricum,* eager to denude the empire of its wealth and stability. The image of this warrior has come down to us through the epigraphic and sculptural record, and more recently archaeological data, to become a fixed point in the modern world's appreciation of the world of Rome. Wearing his *lorica segmentata* and Gallic helmet, *scutum* shield set firm and *gladius* in hand, he has helped define our understanding of warfare in the ancient world.

Yet we have also seen in this book that the legionary was so much more. In the first instance we have come to appreciate his human face, looking at how he was recruited, his terms of service, what he ate, how he campaigned and how he fought. We have also seen the legionary carrying out a myriad of non-conflict related tasks, always the first port of call for the emperor, governor or procurator when the state called them to duty. Such tasks ranged from administering the empire, policing it both without and within, fighting fires, running agriculture and industry, and undertaking engineering and construction. In this latter role we see across the entirety of the empire the fruits of the skill of the legionary as an engineer with the many roads and buildings that still exist today.

Finally, we have considered the legionary as part of the wider Roman military system, never a troop type to operate alone but most often fighting alongside his *auxilia* and naval *milite* counterparts. While such a distinction between the legionary and other troop types was to largely disappear as the empire entered its Dominate phase, units such as the *Iovani* and *Herculiani* maintained the traditional élan which had been so much a part of the legionary experience from the reforms of Marius in the later republic. As we have seen, this martial spirit and expertise of the legionary was to far outlast the decline of the empire in the west, if only in the form of Byzantine *skutatoi,* and our appreciation of the Roman world today.

| **55 BC** | The first Roman invasion of Britain, Julius Caesar's first incursion. |
| **54 BC** | The second Roman invasion of Britain, Julius Caesar's second incursion. |
| **AD 40** | Caligula's planned invasion of Britain aborted. |
| **AD 43** | The third, and successful, Roman invasion of Britain under the Emperor Claudius, with the legionaries, *auxilia* and naval *milites* commanded by Aulus Plautius. |
| **AD 44** | The future Emperor Vespasian successfully campaigns in south-west Britain, leading the legio II Augusta. |
| **AD 47** | Vespasian successfully concludes his campaign to conquer south-west Britain. Governor Publius Ostorius Scapula campaigns in north Wales, also subduing the first revolt by Iceni tribe in north East Anglia. |
| **AD 48** | First revolt of the Brigantes tribe in northern Britain. |
| **AD 50** | Construction begins of first forum in London. |
| **AD 51** | The leader of the British resistance to Roman rule, Caratacus, is captured by the Romans after being handed over by the Brigantian Queen, Cartimandua. |
| **AD 52** | The Silures tribe in southern Wales are pacified by Governor Didius Gallus. |
| **AD 57** | Rome intervenes in favour of Queen Cartimandua in a dispute over the leadership of the Brigantes. |
| **AD 59/60** | The initial subjugation of the Druids in the far west, and the initial invasion of Anglesey by Governor Paulinus. This campaign is cut short by the Boudiccan revolt. |
| **AD 60/61** | The Boudiccan revolt featuring the destruction of Colchester, St Albans and London. The revolt is defeated by Paulinus. |

**AD 69**     Cartimandua, queen of the Brigantes and ally of Rome, is overthrown by former husband Venutius.

**AD 71**     Governor Quintus Petilius Cerialiss campaigns in the north of Britain. The Brigantes are defeated, with Venutius captured and killed.

**AD 74**     Further campaigning in Wales; Chester is founded.

**AD 77**     Gnaeus Julius Agricola becomes the new governor. Wales and western Britain are finally conquered.

**AD 78–82**  Agricola consolidates control of Brigantian territory, and then campaigns to the north and in Scotland.

**AD 83**     Agricola brings the combined Caledonian tribes to battle at Mons Graupius in the Grampians. After his victory the Classis Britannica circumnavigates northern Scotland. The conquest of Britain is declared 'complete', commemorated by a monumental arch at Richborough in modern Kent.

**AD 87**     Roman troops are withdrawn from the far north of Britain because of pressures elsewhere in the empire. The legionary fortress of Inchtuthill in Tayside is abandoned.

**AD 100**    Trajan orders the full withdrawal of Roman troops from Scotland, and then establishes a new frontier along the Solway Firth–Tyne line. All defences north of this line are abandoned by AD 105.

**AD 117**    Major disturbances in the north of the Province of Britannia.

**AD 122**    Emperor Hadrian visits Britain, tasking Governor Aulus Platorius Nepos with the construction of Hadrian's Wall.

**AD 142**    Military engagements north of Hadrian's Wall continue under Quintus Lollius Urbicus, on the orders of Antoninus Pius, in an attempt to subdue the tribes of northern Britain and southern Scotland, the latter region being conquered again. Construction then begins of the Antonine Wall along Clyde–Forth line as a new northern frontier.

**AD 162**    The Antonine Wall is evacuated, with the northern border once again moving south to the line of Hadrian's Wall.

**AD 175**    5,500 Sarmatian cavalry are sent to Britain, perhaps because of a military emergency.

**AD 182**    The tribes either side of Hadrian's Wall start raiding along and across the border, with Roman troops responding with counter-raids. Towns far to the south of the wall begin constructing earth-and-timber defence circuits, indicating that tribal raiding penetrated far into the province.

**AD 184**    Commodus receives his seventh acclamation as imperator, taking the title Britannicus indicating some kind of military victory in the province.

**AD 185**    Some 1,500 picked troops from Britain travel to Rome with a petition for the Emperor Commodus. They ask that he dismisses the Praetorian Prefect Perennis.

**AD 196**    British governor Albinus usurps, invades Gaul and is proclaimed emperor by the legions from Britain and Spain.

**AD 197**    Albinus is defeated by Septimius Severus at Lugdunum (modern Lyons) and is killed. Around the time the province of Britain is divided into Britannia Superior and Britannia Inferior.

**AD 197/198**    Severus sends military commissioners to Britain aiming to quickly suppress the remaining supporters of Albinus. Roman troops rebuild parts of Hadrian's Wall (some of which may have actually been destroyed) and other parts of the northern defences which had been damaged by an increase in tribal raiding after Albinus had travelled to Gaul with his troops. Construction also starts at this time of the land walls of London.

**AD 207**   News arrives in Rome from Britain (perhaps the letter from Senecio detailed by Herodian) asking Severus for urgent assistance in the form of the emperor himself or more troops. He responds with both.

**AD 208**   Severus arrives in Britain with the imperial household and a huge army, he planning a major campaign against the Maeatae and Caledonian tribal confederations north of Hadrian's Wall. St Alban is martyred.

**AD 209**   The first Severan campaign in Scotland.

**AD 210**   The second Severan campaign in Scotland, led by Caracalla. Genocide ordered by Severus.

**AD 211**   Severus dies at York, with his sons Caracalla and Geta becoming joint emperors. The campaign in the north of Britain is suspended. Caracalla murders Geta. Britain is later officially divided into two provinces, Britannia Superior and Britannia Inferior.

**AD 250**   Irish raiding takes place along the west coast, with Germanic raiding along the east coast. The first use of the term Pict to describe the confederation of tribes in northern Scotland.

**AD 260**   The 'Gallic Empire' is declared by Postumus, splitting Britain, Gaul and Spain away from the empire.

**AD 268**   Postumus is murdered by his own troops.

**AD 274**   Emperor Aurelian defeats the 'Gallic Empire', with Britain, Gaul and Spain then rejoining the empire.

**AD 277**   Vandals and Burgundian mercenaries are settled in Britain, with Victorinus defeating a British usurpation.

**AD 287**    The usurpation of Carausius, which splits Britain and northern Gaul away from the empire.

**AD 293**    Carausius is assassinated by Allectus who then takes over control from his former master in Britain.

**AD 296**    The fourth Roman invasion of Britain, with Constantius Chlorus invading to defeat Allectus, the western caesar then returning the two provinces to the empire. Around this time Britain is declared a diocese as part of the Diocletianic Reformation, with the four Provinces of Maxima Caesariensis, Britannia Prima, Flavia Caesariensis and Britannia Secunda.

**AD 306**    Constantius Chlorus campaigns in the north of Britain, then dies in York. His son Constantine is proclaimed emperor by the legionaries of legio VI Victrix.

**AD 343**    Emperor Constans makes a surprise winter crossing of the English Channel to Britain following the defeat of his brother Constantine II three years earlier, possibly in the context of a military emergency in the north of the diocese.

**AD 351**    Constantius II sends Paul 'the chain' to Britain to purge the aristocracy after the revolt of Magnentius. The *vicarius* of the diocese, Martinus, commits suicide rather than face trial.

**AD 359**    British bishops attend the Council of Rimini. Emperor Julian collects and builds 600 ships to transport grain from Britain to feed his Rhine army.

**AD 367**    The 'Great Conspiracy' of Picts from Scotland, Attecotti from the Western Isles, Irish and Germanic raiders attack Britain, overwhelming the frontier defences.

| AD 369 | Count Theodosius arrives in Britain to suppress the revolt and restore order, with Magnus Maximus serving under him. The northern frontier is then rebuilt yet again. |
|---|---|
| AD 383 | Magnus Maximus (now the British military commander, and possibly the vicarius of the diocese) campaigns against Pictish and Irish raiders. He is proclaimed emperor by his troops, then invading Gaul which declares its support for him, as does Spain. |
| AD 387 | Magnus Maximus invades Italy where he ousts Emperor Valentinian II. |
| AD 388 | Magnus Maximus is defeated and executed by Theodosius I, emperor in the East. |
| AD 400 | The Western Empire magister militum Stilicho campaigns in Britain and defeats Pictish, Irish and Germanic raiders. He then withdraws many troops from the diocese to help defend Italy against the Goths, with Britain left dangerously exposed to further attack. |
| AD 405 | Heavy Irish raiding on the south-western coast of Britain, this being a possible date for the capture of St Patrick. |
| AD 407 | In swift succession the military in Britain declare Marcus, then Gratian and finally Constantine III to be the emperor. The latter crosses to Gaul with the remaining *comitatenses* field army troops from Britain, setting up his capital at Arles. The diocese now only has the *limitanei* troops to defend its borders. |
| AD 409 | The British aristocracy throw out their Roman administrators, with the diocese cut adrift from the remaining parts of the Western Empire. |
| AD 410 | The Western Emperor Honorius allegedly tells the Britons to look to their own defences. |
| AD 429 | St Germanus visits Britain to debate with the Pelagian Christians there. Further conflict takes place with Pictish and Irish raiders |
| AD 430 | The effective end of coin use in Britain. |

# SELECT BIBLIOGRAPHY

## PRIMARY SOURCES

Cassius Dio (1925). *Roman History*. Cary, E., Harvard: Loeb Classical Library.

Cornelius Tacitus (1970). *The Agricola.* Mattingly, H., London: Penguin.

Herodian (1989). *History of the Roman Empire.* Whittaker, C. R., Harvard: Loeb Classical Library.

Julius Caesar (1951). *The Conquest of Gaul.* Handford, S.A., London: Penguin.

Polybius (1979). *The Rise of the Roman Empire.* Scott-Kilvert, I., London: Penguin.

Sextus Julius (1969). *Frontinus, Strategemata.* Bennett, C.E., Portsmouth, New Hampshire: Heinemann.

Suetonius (1937). *The Twelve Caesars.* Graves, R., London: Penguin.

## SECONDARY SOURCES

Bidwell, P. (2007). *Roman Forts in Britain.* Stroud: Tempus.

Birley, A. R. (1999). *Septimius Severus: The African Emperor.* Abingdon: Routledge.

Breeze, D. J. and Dobson, B. (2000). *Hadrian's Wall.* London: Penguin.

Burnham, B. C. and Davies, J. L. (2010). *Roman Frontiers in Wales and the Marches.* Aberystwyth: Royal Commission on the Ancient and Historical Monuments of Wales.

Connolly, P. (1988). *Greece and Rome at War.* London: Macdonald & Co (Publishers) Ltd.

Cornell, T. J. and Matthews, J. (1982). *Atlas of the Roman World.* Oxford: Phaidon Press Ltd.

Cowan, R. (2003). *Roman Legionary, 58 BC–AD 69.* Oxford: Osprey Publishing.

Cowan, R. (2003). *Imperial Roman Legionary, AD 161–284.* Oxford, Osprey Publishing.

Cowan, R. (2015). *Roman Legionary AD 284-337*. Oxford: Osprey Publishing.

D'Amato, R. (2009). *Imperial Roman Naval Forces 31BC–AD500*. Oxford: Osprey Publishing.

D'Amato, R. and Sumner, G. (2009). *Arms and Armour of the Imperial Roman Soldier*. Barnsley: Frontline Books.

Elliott, P. (2014). *Legions in Crisis*. Stroud: Fonthill Media ltd.

Elliott, S. (2016). *Sea Eagles to Empire: The Classis Britannica and the Battles for Britain*. Stroud: The History Press.

Elliott, S. (2017). *Empire State: How the Roman Military Built an Empire*. Oxford: Oxbow Books.

Esmonde Cleary, A. S. (2013). *The Roman West AD 200–500*. Cambridge: Cambridge University Press.

Faulkner, N. (2001). *The Decline and Fall of Roman Britain*. Stroud: Tempus.

Fields, N. (2006). *Rome's Saxon Shore.* Oxford: Osprey Publishing.

Goldsworthy, A. (2000). *Roman Warfare*. London: Cassell.

Goldsworthy, A. (2003). *The Complete Roman Army.* London: Thames and Hudson.

Grainge, G. (2005). *The Roman Invasions of Britain.* Stroud: Tempus.

James, S. (2011). *Rome and the Sword.* London: Thames and Hudson.

Jones, B. and Mattingly, D. (1990). *An Atlas of Roman Britain*. Oxford: Oxbow Books.

Jones, R. (2012). *Roman Marching Camps in Britain.* Storud: Amberley Publishing.

Kamm, A. (2011). *The Last Frontier: The Roman Invasions of Scotland*. Glasgow: Tempus.

Kiley, K. F. (2012). *The Uniforms of the Roman World*. Wigston: Lorenz Books.

Le Bohec, Y. (2000). *The Imperial Roman Army*. London: Routledge.

Mattingly, D. (2006). *An Imperial Possession, Britain in the Roman Empire.* London: Penguin.

Moorhead, S. and Stuttard, D. (2012). *The Romans Who Shaped Britain.* London: Thames and Hudson.

Scarre, C. (1995). *The Penguin Historical Atlas of Ancient Rome.* London: Penguin.

Scarre, C. (1995). *Chronicle of the Roman Emperors*: London: Thames and Hudson.

Whitby, M. (2002). *Rome at War AD 293–696*. Oxford: Osprey Publishing.

# ACKNOWLEDGEMENTS

I would like to thank those who have helped make this appreciation of the Roman legionary possible. Firstly, as always, Professor Andrew Lambert of the War Studies Department at KCL, Dr Andrew Gardner at UCL's Institute of Archaeology and Dr Steve Willis at the University of Kent. All continue to encourage my research on the Roman military. Next, my publisher Clare Litt at Casemate. Also Professor Sir Barry Cunliffe of the School of Archaeology at Oxford University, and Professor Martin Millett at the Faculty of Classics, Cambridge University. Finally my patient proof reader and lovely wife Sara. All have contributed greatly and freely, enabling this work on the Roman legionary to reach fruition. Finally of course, I would like to thank my family, especially Sara once again, and my children Alex and Lizzie.

Thank you all,

Dr Simon Elliott
February 2018

# INDEX